The Mystery of Night Dreams

Unraveling the Symbols and Messages in Your Sleep

Ellie Bloom

Contents

Chapter 1

Introduction

Unveiling the Mystique of Dreams

In the quiet corners of our minds, when the world slips into the hushed embrace of night, dreams unfurl their enchanting tapestry. Dreams, those ephemeral wanderings of the mind, have captivated humanity since time immemorial, leaving an indelible mark on the pages of history and the echoes of our collective consciousness. They are the silent storytellers of the night, weaving narratives that dance between the realms of fantasy and reality. In this journey through the corridors of the unconscious mind, we embark on an exploration of the allure of dreams, their historical significance, and the timeless quest to interpret the enigmatic messages they bear.

The Allure of Dreams: A Gateway to the Unconscious

Dreams possess an irresistible allure, drawing us into a realm where the ordinary transforms into the extraordinary, and the mundane is overshadowed by the extraordinary. The allure of dreams lies in their ability to transport us beyond the boundaries of waking reality, offering a glimpse into the deepest recesses of our minds. In this realm, the laws of physics yield to the whims of imagination, and the boundaries of time and space dissolve into a surreal landscape where anything is possible.

From the earliest civilizations to the present day, dreams have been revered as portals to the divine, glimpses into the future, and mirrors reflecting the innermost thoughts and desires of the dreamer. Ancient cultures often believed that dreams were messages from the gods or ancestors, and their interpretation held the key to unlocking hidden truths and guiding individuals through the labyrinth of life. The allure of dreams, steeped in mysticism and symbolism, has persisted through the ages, transcending cultural and temporal boundaries.

A Brief Overview of Dream Interpretation Through the Ages

As we trace the historical trajectory of dream interpretation, we encounter a rich tapestry woven with threads of philosophy, religion, and psychology. The ancient Egyptians, for example, placed immense importance on dreams, considering them as direct communication from the divine. The Egyptians documented their dreams on papyrus, believing that unraveling the symbolism within these nocturnal visions held the key to understanding the will of the gods.

In ancient Greece, dreams were often viewed through the lens of divine intervention as well. The influential philosopher Aristotle proposed that dreams were the result of the mind attempting to make sense of sensory stimuli encountered throughout the day. His ideas, though rooted in the physical world, acknowledged the profound impact dreams had on the human psyche.

The medieval period witnessed a shift in perspective, with dreams becoming battlegrounds for spiritual warfare. Theologians such as St.

Augustine grappled with the dichotomy of dreams as either divine messages or temptations from malevolent forces. The interpretation of dreams became entwined with moral and religious considerations, influencing the conduct of individuals in waking life.

Fast forward to the 20th century, and the realm of dream interpretation underwent a revolution with the advent of psychoanalysis. Sigmund Freud, the pioneering figure in the field, proposed that dreams were the "royal road to the unconscious." Freud's theories delved into the symbolic language of dreams, positing that their content held clues to repressed desires, unresolved conflicts, and the intricate workings of the human psyche.

Carl Jung, Freud's contemporary and collaborator turned critic, introduced the concept of the collective unconscious and archetypes, expanding the scope of dream analysis beyond the individual to encompass universal symbols and themes. The landscape of dream interpretation evolved further, incorporating elements of cultural and personal significance.

What Readers Can Expect to Learn and Discover About Their Own Dreams

As we embark on this exploration together, readers can anticipate a transformative journey into the heart of their dreams—a journey that transcends time, culture, and individual experience. The pages that follow will serve as a guide, offering insight into the symbolic language of dreams and providing tools to decode the messages that lie beneath the surface of our nocturnal wanderings.

In the chapters ahead, we will delve into the multifaceted nature of dreams, unraveling common symbols that thread through the tapestry of our collective unconscious. From the thrill of flying through boundless skies to the disconcerting freefall into the abyss, each dream holds a mirror to our innermost fears, desires, and aspirations.

The journey will not only be one of introspection but also one of practical application. Dream journals, mindfulness techniques, and the art of lucid dreaming will be unveiled as invaluable tools to enhance your connection with the dream world. By cultivating awareness and actively engaging with your dreams, you will unlock the doors to self-discovery, creativity, and personal growth.

Nightmares, often dismissed as mere nocturnal disturbances, will be reframed as powerful messengers bearing gifts of insight and opportunities for cathartic transformation. Through the exploration of nightmares, you will learn to confront fears, confront unresolved issues, and harness the latent potential for healing that dreams can offer.

The concept of dream work, including shared dreaming and interpreting signs within the dream realm, will be explored as bridges connecting the individual to the collective consciousness. Your dreams, it will be revealed, are not isolated phenomena but interconnected threads in the rich tapestry of the human experience.

In the grand finale of our journey, we will explore the realm of lucid dreaming—a state in which you become the architect of your dreams, navigating through the landscapes of your own creation. This powerful tool, when harnessed, opens up new dimensions for self-exploration, empowerment, and the manifestation of your deepest aspirations.

As you turn the pages of "The Mystery of Night Dreams," be prepared to unravel the secrets, unlock the wisdom, and embrace the transformative power that resides within the hidden recesses of your sleep. Together, we will embark on a voyage through the realms of the unconscious, unveiling the mysteries that have lingered in the shadows of the night for centuries. Sweet dreams await, and with them, the promise of self-discovery and a more fulfilling life.

Chapter 2

The Science of Dreaming

In the quietude of night, as the world around us succumbs to the gentle embrace of slumber, a symphony of neural activity unfolds within the recesses of the brain. Dreams, those enigmatic narratives that play out in the theater of our minds during sleep, are not mere specters of the imagination but rather intricate manifestations of the brain's nocturnal choreography. In this chapter, we embark on a journey into the labyrinth of the sleeping brain, seeking to unravel the intricacies of the science of dreaming—exploring what happens in the brain during sleep, the different stages of sleep, and the latest research shedding light on the profound question of why we dream.

Understanding What Happens in the Brain During Sleep

The brain, that organ of ceaseless activity and perpetual curiosity, undergoes a profound transformation as it transitions from wakefulness to sleep. As we delve into the science of dreaming, it is essential to first comprehend the intricate dance of neurotransmitters, hormones, and neural networks that orchestrates the transition between wakefulness and slumber.

The journey begins in the brainstem, a primal region responsible for regulating essential functions such as breathing and heart rate. Here, the reticular activating system (RAS) acts as a gatekeeper, controlling the flow of information into the brain. As external stimuli diminish during the descent into sleep, the RAS gradually releases its grip, allowing the cerebral cortex—the outer layer of the brain responsible for conscious thought and perception—to enter a state of reduced activity.

Simultaneously, a neurotransmitter known as adenosine accumulates in the brain throughout the waking hours. The build-up of adenosine creates a mounting pressure for sleep. When we finally succumb to the urge to rest, adenosine receptors are activated, initiating the descent into the initial stages of sleep.

As the transition to sleep unfolds, the brain traverses through various states, each characterized by distinct patterns of neural activity. Electroencephalography (EEG) recordings reveal these fluctuations, marking the passage through wakefulness, light sleep, deep sleep, and the crown jewel of our exploration—the rapid eye movement (REM) stage, where dreams come to life.

The Different Stages of Sleep and Where Dreams Occur

The sleep cycle, a rhythmic oscillation between different stages, repeats approximately every 90 to 110 minutes throughout the night. Understanding these stages is pivotal to unraveling the science of dreaming, as each phase plays a unique role in shaping the nocturnal experience.

NREM Stage 1: As we drift from wakefulness to sleep, the brain enters the initial phase of non-rapid eye movement (NREM) sleep. Lasting only a few minutes, this stage is a transitional state where the body begins to relax, and hypnagogic hallucinations may occur—brief, dream-like experiences.

NREM Stage 2: Progressing further, NREM Stage 2 is characterized by a reduction in heart rate and a decrease in body temperature. Sleep spindles and K-complexes, distinctive EEG patterns, emerge during this stage, contributing to the maintenance of stable sleep.

NREM Stages 3 and 4 (Deep Sleep): These stages mark the onset of deep sleep, where the body undergoes vital restoration and repair. Growth hormone is released, promoting physical rejuvenation, and the brain engages in memory consolidation. Dreams are less prevalent in these stages, and if awakened, individuals often report a sense of disorientation.

REM Stage: The jewel in the crown of the sleep cycle, REM sleep is where dreams most vividly manifest. Characterized by rapid eye movements, heightened brain activity, and a temporary paralysis of voluntary muscles (known as REM atonia), this stage is a playground for the surreal. It is during REM sleep that the most memorable and intense dreams occur, captivating the dreamer in a realm where logic and reality intertwine.

Understanding the cyclic nature of these sleep stages provides a framework for comprehending the ebb and flow of dreaming throughout the night. The brain, a master conductor orchestrating the symphony of sleep, navigates through these stages, sculpting the landscape where dreams unfurl their ethereal narratives.

The Latest Research on Why We Dream

The age-old question of why we dream has spurred countless theories, from the mystical interpretations of ancient civilizations to the psychoanalytic musings of Freud and Jung. In recent years, advancements in neuroscience and sleep research have shed new light on this profound mystery, offering insights into the purpose and function of dreaming.

Memory Consolidation: One prominent theory suggests that dreams play a crucial role in memory consolidation. During REM sleep, the brain actively processes and integrates information acquired throughout the day, strengthening synaptic connections and facilitating the transfer of short-term memories to long-term storage. This perspective posits that dreaming serves as a form of cognitive housekeeping, optimizing the brain's capacity to learn and adapt.

Emotional Regulation: Another line of research emphasizes the role of dreaming in emotional regulation. Dreams, particularly those occurring during REM sleep, often feature emotionally charged scenarios. It is proposed that these dream experiences provide a platform for the brain to process and regulate intense emotions, helping individuals cope with stress, trauma, and unresolved psychological conflicts.

Problem Solving and Creativity: Dreams have been lauded as fertile grounds for problem-solving and creative insight. The surreal, non-linear nature of dream narratives may facilitate the exploration of unconventional solutions to real-world challenges. Creatives throughout history, from artists to scientists, have credited dreams with inspiring breakthroughs and innovative ideas.

Threat Simulation: Evolutionary perspectives posit that dreaming evolved as a mechanism for simulating threatening scenarios. By mentally rehearsing potential dangers during sleep, our ancestors may have enhanced their survival instincts and preparedness for challenges in the waking world. This theory aligns with the prevalence of dreams featuring scenarios of pursuit, danger, and escape.

Neurological Maintenance: Dreams may also serve as a form of neurological maintenance, allowing the brain to prune unnecessary connections and optimize its neural network. This theory aligns with the observation that infants, who experience a higher proportion of REM sleep, may utilize dreaming as a mechanism for fine-tuning their developing brains.

While these theories offer compelling insights into the potential functions of dreaming, it's crucial to note that the science of dreaming remains a vibrant and evolving field. The multifaceted nature of dreams may defy singular explanations, and ongoing research continues to unravel the intricate tapestry of nocturnal cognition.

Navigating the Dreamscapes of the Mind

As we conclude our exploration into the science of dreaming, we emerge with a newfound appreciation for the orchestration of the sleeping brain. From the dance of neurotransmitters that usher us into slumber to the vivid narratives that play out in the theater of REM sleep, the science of dreaming unveils the profound intricacies of the nocturnal mind.

Our journey through the different stages of sleep has illuminated the cyclical nature of the sleep cycle, with each phase contributing to the restorative and transformative processes that unfold during the night. Dreams, like transient echoes of the unconscious, manifest most vividly during REM sleep, providing a canvas for the mind to explore, process, and create.

In contemplating the latest research on why we dream, we find ourselves standing at the crossroads of scientific inquiry and the enduring mysteries of the human experience. Theories surrounding memory consolidation, emotional regulation, problem-solving

Chapter 3

A Brief History of Dream Interpretation

In the vast tapestry of human history, dreams have been both revered and feared, interpreted as omens, messages from the divine, or windows into the recesses of the unconscious mind. As we embark on a journey through time, we will unravel the threads of dream interpretation, exploring the views of ancient civilizations, delving into the groundbreaking contributions of key figures like Freud and Jung, and tracing the evolution of dream analysis across the ages.

Ancient Civilizations and Their Views on Dreams

Long before the emergence of modern psychology, ancient civilizations held profound beliefs about the significance of dreams. For many, the dream realm was a sacred space, a conduit between the mortal and the divine. In these early interpretations, dreams were considered messages from the gods, offering guidance, warnings, or glimpses into the future.

Ancient Egypt: Ancient Egypt revered dreams as sacred channels of divine communication. Believing them to be direct messages from the gods, Egyptians attributed great significance to their nocturnal visions. Dream interpretation, a skill honed by priests and priestesses, was considered a sacred art. These interpreters, serving as intermediaries between mortals and the divine, delved into the symbolic meanings of dreams, drawing from religious texts and oracles to decipher their messages.

In this ancient civilization, dreams were not merely random figments of the imagination; they were revered as prophetic glimpses into the future. Pharaohs and rulers often relied on dreams to guide their decisions, trusting in their predictive powers to shape the destiny of their kingdom. Dream incubation, a ritual practice, involved seeking guidance or healing through dreams by sleeping in sacred temples or shrines dedicated to specific deities. Through purification rites, prayers, and offerings, individuals sought to invoke divine visions during sleep.

Symbolism and allegory permeated Egyptian dream interpretation. Each element within a dream was laden with deeper meaning, reflecting the individual's life, destiny, or spiritual journey. Animals, plants, and celestial bodies carried specific significance, interpreted based on their cultural associations and mythological narratives.

Ancient Egyptian religious texts and mythology are replete with references to dreams. The "Book of the Dead" and the "Instructions of Ptahhotep" contain passages that underscore the importance of dreams as conduits of divine communication and preparation for the afterlife. Dreams were integral to religious rituals, serving as a link between the mortal world and the realm of the gods.

Dreams were also viewed as preparatory journeys for the soul's passage into the afterlife. Believing in an existence beyond death, Egyptians saw dreams as guiding souls through the trials and tribulations of the underworld. Dreams offered insights into the soul's journey and provided solace to the bereaved, reassuring them of their loved ones' continued existence in the afterlife.

Ancient Greece: In ancient Greece, dreams held a significant place in both religious and philosophical thought, shaping beliefs about the nature of reality, the human psyche, and the divine. Unlike the Egyptians, who viewed dreams primarily as messages from the gods, the Greeks approached dreams with a blend of reverence, skepticism, and curiosity.

One of the earliest recorded accounts of dream interpretation in Greek literature comes from the epic poems of Homer, particularly the "Iliad" and the "Odyssey." In these texts, dreams are portrayed as divine messages that can reveal glimpses of the future or provide guidance to mortals. Characters such as Agamemnon and Penelope receive prophetic dreams that foreshadow future events, underscoring the belief in the prophetic power of dreams.

The ancient Greeks attributed dreams to a variety of sources, including the influence of gods and goddesses, the machinations of supernatural beings such as daimons, and the inner workings of the human mind. One of the most famous examples of divine dream intervention in Greek mythology is the story of King Croesus of Lydia, who received a prophetic dream warning him of the downfall of his kingdom. Despite this warning, Croesus misinterpreted the dream and ultimately suffered a tragic fate, illustrating the complexities of dream interpretation in Greek culture.

Greek philosophers such as Plato and Aristotle offered their own theories on dreams, incorporating them into broader discussions about the nature of consciousness, the soul, and reality. Plato, in his dialogue "Theaetetus," explores the idea of dreams as a reflection of the soul's experiences and desires, suggesting that they offer insights into the inner workings of the psyche. Aristotle, on the other hand, viewed dreams as a natural phenomenon arising from the sensory experiences of the waking state, dismissing the idea of divine intervention in favor of a more rational explanation.

Dreams also played a role in religious practices and rituals in ancient Greece. Temples dedicated to healing gods such as Asclepius were renowned for their use of dream incubation as a form of divine healing. Pilgrims would travel to these sanctuaries seeking guidance and cure through dreams, believing that the gods would communicate with them during sleep and offer remedies for physical and spiritual ailments.

Theater and literature in ancient Greece often incorporated dream imagery and themes, exploring the subconscious mind and its influence on human behavior. Greek tragedies such as Euripides' "Medea" and Sophocles' "Oedipus Rex" feature characters haunted by prophetic dreams that foretell their tragic fates, highlighting the tension between fate and free will in Greek mythology.

Mesopotamia: In ancient Mesopotamia, dreams held a profound significance, serving as powerful messages from the divine realm and influencing various aspects of society, religion, and governance. Mesopotamian civilizations, including the Sumerians, Akkadians, Babylonians, and Assyrians, believed that dreams were a means of communication between mortals and the gods, providing insights into the future, guidance in decision-making, and revelations about the human condition.

One of the earliest recorded instances of dream interpretation in Mesopotamian history can be found in the Epic of Gilgamesh, one of the oldest literary works in the world. In this epic poem, Gilgamesh, the legendary king of Uruk, receives prophetic dreams foretelling the arrival of his companion and future rival, Enkidu. These dreams, interpreted by his mother, Ninsun, serve as harbingers of the epic journey that Gilgamesh is destined to undertake, illustrating the belief in the prophetic power of dreams among the ancient Mesopotamians.

Dream interpretation was a specialized skill practiced by priests and seers known as "baru" or "bārû" who served as intermediaries between the gods and the people. These priests, trained in the art of divination, would analyze the content and symbolism of dreams to discern their meanings and offer guidance to those seeking answers or insights. Dream omens were recorded in extensive catalogs known as dream books or "Oneiromancies," which provided interpretations for a wide range of dream scenarios based on religious and cultural symbolism.

The ancient Mesopotamians believed that dreams were sent by the gods to convey messages, warnings, or instructions to mortals. Kings and rulers often consulted dream interpreters before making impor-tant decisions, seeking guidance from the gods on matters of statecraft, warfare, and governance. Dreams were seen as a form of divine guidance, offering insights into the will of the gods and the fate of individuals and nations.

Dreams also played a role in religious rituals and ceremonies in Mesopotamia, where they were used to communicate with the gods and seek divine favor. Temples dedicated to specific deities, such as the temple of the god Shamash in the city of Larsa, were renowned for their use of dream divination as a form of healing and prophecy. Pilgrims would travel to these sacred sites seeking guidance and blessings through dreams, believing that the gods would communicate with them during sleep and offer solutions to their problems or ailments.

Mesopotamian art and literature often depicted dream imagery and themes, reflecting the cultural importance of dreams in society. Cylinder seals, reliefs, and other artifacts from ancient Mesopotamia frequently feature scenes of dreamers encountering divine beings or receiving messages from the gods in their dreams. The "Dream of Dumuzid," a Sumerian poem, recounts the story of the shepherd-god Dumuzid's dream visitation by his deceased sister, Geshtinanna, offering insights into the Mesopotamian beliefs about the afterlife and the role of dreams in religious experience.

Significant Figures in the History of Dream Analysis

As we transition to more recent epochs, we encounter pivotal figures whose contributions laid the foundations for modern dream analysis. These visionaries delved into the depths of the human psyche, pioneering theories that shaped the landscape of dream interpretation.

Sigmund Freud (1856-1939): Sigmund Freud, the Austrian neurologist and founder of psychoanalysis, made groundbreaking contributions to the field of dream interpretation with his seminal work, "The Interpretation of Dreams," published in 1899. Freud's theories revolutionized the understanding of dreams, positing that they are the royal road to the unconscious mind and a key to unlocking repressed desires, conflicts, and memories.

Central to Freud's theory of dream interpretation is the concept of the unconscious mind, which he believed harbored hidden desires, fears, and unresolved conflicts that influence thoughts, feelings, and behaviors. According to Freud, dreams serve as a form of wish fulfillment, allowing individuals to gratify unconscious wishes and desires that are repressed or suppressed in waking life. Dreams, therefore, provide a window into the deepest recesses of the psyche, revealing hidden aspects of the self that are inaccessible to conscious awareness.

Freud distinguished between the manifest content and the latent content of dreams. The manifest content refers to the literal storyline and imagery of the dream as recalled by the dreamer, while the latent content represents the underlying symbolic meanings and unconscious wishes concealed within the dream. Freud argued that dreams are symbolic in nature, disguising forbidden or taboo desires in metaphorical imagery to evade censorship by the conscious mind.

Freud identified several common dream symbols and motifs, such as falling, flying, nudity, and teeth falling out, which he interpreted as representations of primal urges, sexual fantasies, and unresolved conflicts. For example, Freud interpreted dreams of flying as symbolic expressions of the desire for freedom and sexual release, while dreams of teeth falling out were seen as manifestations of castration anxiety or fear of impotence.

Freud also proposed the concept of dream work, a process by which the unconscious mind transforms latent wishes into manifest content through a series of mechanisms, including condensation, displacement, symbolization, and secondary revision. Condensation involves the merging of multiple thoughts, feelings, or images into a single dream element, while displacement entails the transfer of emotional significance from one object or person to another. Symbolization involves the substitution of symbolic representations for forbidden or taboo desires, while secondary revision refers to the process by which the dream is elaborated and distorted in the act of waking recollection.

Freud's psychoanalytic approach to dream interpretation has had a profound influence on psychology, psychiatry, and cultural discourse, shaping our understanding of the unconscious mind and the symbolic language of dreams. While his theories have been subject to criticism and revision over the years, Freud's emphasis on the importance of dreams as a means of accessing the unconscious psyche continues to resonate with scholars and clinicians today. Freud's legacy as the father of modern dream interpretation endures, leaving an indelible mark on the study of human consciousness and behavior.

Carl Jung (1875-1961): Carl Gustav Jung, the Swiss psychiatrist and founder of analytical psychology, made significant contributions to the field of dream interpretation, building upon the work of Sigmund Freud and advancing a more holistic and symbolic approach to understanding dreams. Jung's theories emphasized the role of the unconscious mind, archetypal symbols, and the collective unconscious in shaping dreams and personal growth.

Central to Jung's theory of dream interpretation is the concept of the collective unconscious, a reservoir of shared psychological material inherited from ancestral experiences and universal human experiences. According to Jung, the collective unconscious contains a vast array of archetypes, or primordial symbols and motifs that are common to all cultures and societies. These archetypes manifest in dreams as universal symbols and themes, reflecting fundamental aspects of the human psyche.

Jung proposed that dreams serve a compensatory function, balancing conscious attitudes and behaviors with unconscious desires and conflicts. Dreams, therefore, offer insights into the individual's psychological state and point towards areas of personal growth and development. Jung believed that the symbols and images that appear in dreams are not arbitrary but are imbued with personal and collective meaning, reflecting the individual's innermost thoughts, feelings, and experiences.

Unlike Freud, who focused primarily on the individual's personal unconscious and repressed desires, Jung emphasized the importance of the collective unconscious and archetypal symbols in dream interpretation. Jung argued that dreams provide a bridge between the conscious and unconscious mind, allowing individuals to access deeper layers of the psyche and connect with universal themes and motifs.

Jung identified several key archetypes that commonly appear in dreams, including the anima/animus, the shadow, the persona, and the self. The anima/animus represents the feminine or masculine aspect of the psyche, serving as a symbol of the unconscious opposite gender qualities. The shadow represents the dark, repressed aspects of the self that are often projected onto others, while the persona represents the social mask or facade that individuals present to the world. The self, the central archetype, represents the totality of the psyche and the process of individuation, or the integration of conscious and unconscious elements of the personality.

Jung also introduced the concept of dream symbols and their significance in dream interpretation. He argued that symbols in dreams are not fixed or static but are multifaceted and can have multiple layers of meaning. Jung proposed that dreams should be interpreted holistically, taking into account the context, personal associations, and cultural significance of the symbols and images that appear.

Jung's approach to dream interpretation has had a profound influence on psychology, psychotherapy, and cultural studies, inspiring scholars and clinicians to explore the deeper meaning of dreams and their role in personal transformation and self-discovery. Jung's emphasis on the symbolic language of dreams and the collective unconscious has expanded our understanding of the human psyche and opened new avenues for exploring the mysteries of consciousness and the unconscious mind. His legacy as a pioneer in dream interpretation continues to shape the field of psychology and inspire individuals to explore the depths of their own dreams and inner worlds.

J. Allan Hobson (1933-present): J. Allan Hobson, a prominent American psychiatrist and neuroscientist, has made significant contributions to the field of dream interpretation through his groundbreaking research on the neurobiology of dreaming. Unlike Freud and Jung, who focused on the psychological and symbolic aspects of dreams, Hobson approached dream interpretation from a neuroscientific perspective, seeking to uncover the underlying mechanisms and brain processes involved in dreaming.

Hobson's research challenged traditional views of dreams as manifestations of unconscious desires or symbolic representations of the psyche. Instead, he proposed that dreams are a product of the brain's intrinsic activity, arising from the complex interplay of neuronal networks and neurotransmitter systems during sleep. Through a series of pioneering studies using neuroimaging techniques, animal models, and clinical observations, Hobson revolutionized our understanding of the physiological basis of dreaming.

One of Hobson's most influential contributions to dream interpretation is the activation-synthesis theory, which he developed in collaboration with colleague Robert McCarley in the 1970s. According to this theory, dreams are the result of the brain's attempt to make sense of random neural activity occurring during REM (rapid eye movement) sleep, the stage of sleep associated with vivid dreaming. Hobson and McCarley proposed that the brainstem, particularly the locus coeruleus and raphe nuclei, generates chaotic signals that stimulate the cerebral cortex, leading to the creation of dream imagery and narratives.

The activation-synthesis theory challenged Freudian and Jungian interpretations of dreams, which emphasized the role of unconscious desires, symbolism, and archetypal motifs. Instead, Hobson argued that dreams are a byproduct of the brain's intrinsic activity, devoid of hidden meanings or symbolic significance. According to Hobson, the bizarre and nonsensical nature of dreams reflects the random firing of neurons in the brainstem, rather than deliberate expressions of unconscious wishes or fears.

Hobson's research also shed light on the relationship between dreaming and mental health, particularly in the context of psychiatric disorders such as depression, schizophrenia, and PTSD (post-traumatic stress disorder). He proposed that disturbances in the neurotransmitter systems involved in regulating REM sleep, such as serotonin and noradrenaline, could contribute to the emergence of abnormal dream experiences and emotional disturbances in psychiatric patients.

In addition to his scientific contributions, Hobson has been an influential advocate for the integration of neuroscience and psychology in the study of consciousness and cognition. He has authored numerous books and articles aimed at a general audience, including "The Dreaming Brain" and "Dreaming: An Introduction to the Science of Sleep." Through his writing and lectures, Hobson has sought to bridge the gap between neuroscience and dream interpretation, fostering a greater understanding of the biological basis of dreaming among scientists, clinicians, and the public.

Overall, J. Allan Hobson's pioneering research has transformed our understanding of dream interpretation by emphasizing the neurobiological underpinnings of dreaming. His activation-synthesis theory challenged traditional psychoanalytic views of dreams and paved the way for a more scientifically informed approach to understanding the mysteries of the sleeping mind. Hobson's work continues to inspire researchers and clinicians to explore the intricate relationship between the brain, consciousness, and the enigmatic world of dreams.

Rosalind Cartwright (1922-2002): Rosalind Cartwright, an American psychologist and sleep researcher, has made significant contributions to the field of dream interpretation through her pioneering work on the role of dreams in emotional processing, problem-solving, and mental health. With a career spanning several decades, Cartwright's research has shed light on the complex relationship between dreaming, cognition, and emotional well-being, offering new insights into the function and significance of dreams in human psychology.

One of Cartwright's most notable contributions to dream interpretation is her research on the function of dreams in emotional regulation and coping with stress. Cartwright proposed that dreams serve as a mechanism for processing and integrating emotional experiences, allowing individuals to confront and resolve unresolved conflicts or traumatic memories during sleep. Through a series of empirical studies, including longitudinal research on bereavement and divorce, Cartwright demonstrated that dreams can play a therapeutic role in helping individuals cope with loss, trauma, and emotional distress.

Cartwright's research also challenged traditional psychoanalytic views of dreams as manifestations of repressed desires or symbolic representations of unconscious conflicts. Instead, she argued that dreams are a natural and adaptive process that facilitates emotional processing and problem-solving. According to Cartwright, dreams provide a safe space for exploring difficult emotions and working through unresolved issues, leading to increased psychological resilience and well-being.

In addition to her work on emotional processing, Cartwright has investigated the role of dreams in memory consolidation and cognitive function. She proposed that dreaming may play a role in memory consolidation, particularly for emotionally charged or personally significant experiences. Cartwright's research suggested that dreams may enhance learning and memory by reactivating and reorganizing neural networks during sleep, leading to improved cognitive performance and problem-solving abilities.

Cartwright's research has also highlighted the importance of studying dreams in the context of sleep disorders and mental health conditions. She conducted pioneering studies on the relationship between dreaming and depression, demonstrating that changes in dream content and frequency are associated with depressive symptoms and treatment outcomes. Cartwright's research suggested that alterations in dreaming patterns may serve as early indicators of mood disturbances and provide valuable insights into the underlying mechanisms of depression.

In addition to her empirical research, Cartwright has been a vocal advocate for the integration of dream analysis into clinical practice and psychotherapy. She has authored numerous books and articles aimed at both professional and lay audiences, including "The Twenty-four Hour Mind" and "Crisis Dreaming: Using Your Dreams to Solve Your Problems." Through her writing and lectures, Cartwright has sought to promote a greater understanding of the therapeutic potential of dreams and their role in promoting emotional well-being.

Overall, Rosalind Cartwright's pioneering research has significantly advanced our understanding of dream interpretation and the function of dreams in human psychology. Her work has challenged traditional views of dreams as mere manifestations of unconscious desires and highlighted the adaptive role of dreaming in emotional processing, memory consolidation, and problem-solving. Cartwright's research continues to inspire researchers and clinicians to explore the complex relationship between dreams, cognition, and emotional health, fostering new insights into the mysteries of the sleeping mind.

How Dream Interpretation Has Evolved Over Time

The evolution of dream interpretation reflects not only advancements in scientific understanding but also shifts in cultural, philosophical, and psychological paradigms. While ancient civilizations sought divine guidance in dreams, the advent of psychoanalysis in the late 19th century introduced a more psychological and introspective approach.

Psychoanalytic Era: Freud's psychoanalytic approach dominated the early 20th century, influencing not only psychology but also popular culture. Dream analysis became a cornerstone of psychotherapy, providing a window into the unconscious conflicts that shaped an individual's thoughts and behaviors. Freud's methods, including free association and dream symbolism, became integral to therapeutic practices.

Jungian Expansion: Carl Jung's departure from Freud's theories expanded the scope of dream interpretation. Jung introduced the idea of the collective unconscious, suggesting that dreams tapped into a shared reservoir of archetypal symbols. Analyzing dreams through the lens of archetypes allowed for a broader and more culturally inclusive approach to understanding the human psyche.

Cognitive Revolution: The latter half of the 20th century witnessed the rise of cognitive psychology, challenging some of the more abstract and symbolic interpretations of dreams. Researchers explored the cognitive processes involved in dream formation, emphasizing the role of memory, problem-solving, and emotional regulation. This shift brought a more empirical and scientific lens to the study of dreams.

Neuroscientific Advances: With advancements in neuroimaging technology, the 21st century has seen a surge in neuroscientific research on dreaming. Researchers like J. Allan Hobson have explored the neural mechanisms underlying dream generation, offering insights into the brain's activity during different sleep stages. This convergence of psychology and neuroscience has provided a more comprehensive understanding of the physiological basis of dreams.

Integration of Cultural Perspectives: Contemporary approaches to dream interpretation increasingly recognize the cultural and individual nuances that shape dream symbolism. Dreams are viewed not only as products of universal psychological processes but also as reflections of personal experiences, cultural influences, and societal contexts. This inclusive perspective acknowledges that the meaning of a dream can vary widely based on the dreamer's background and lived experiences.

Navigating the Dreamscape Across Eras

As we traverse the historical landscapes of dream interpretation, we witness the ebb and flow of beliefs, theories, and paradigms. From the mysticism of ancient civilizations to the psychoanalytic revolutions of Freud and Jung, the study of dreams has evolved, embracing scientific inquiry, interdisciplinary perspectives, and cultural sensitivity.

Chapter 4

Common Dream Themes and Their Meanings

Dreams have been a source of fascination and intrigue for millennia, captivating the human imagination with their mysterious symbols, narratives, and emotions. Across cultures and throughout history, certain themes and motifs have recurred in dreams, reflecting universal human experiences, fears, desires, and aspirations. In this chapter, we will explore some of the most common dream themes and their potential meanings, drawing upon psychological research, cultural symbolism, and personal experiences to illuminate the rich tapestry of the dreaming mind.

Flying:

Freedom and Liberation: Dreams of flying often symbolize a desire for freedom, autonomy, and transcendence. The sensation of soaring through the air represents a sense of liberation from constraints, obstacles, or limitations in waking life.

Empowerment and Confidence: Flying dreams can also reflect feelings of empowerment, confidence, and self-assurance. The ability to defy gravity and navigate the skies represents a sense of mastery and control over one's circumstances.

Spiritual Growth and Transcendence: Flying dreams may carry spiritual connotations, symbolizing the soul's journey towards enlightenment, transcendence, or higher states of consciousness. The experience of soaring above earthly concerns represents a longing for spiritual awakening and transcendence.

Example: Sarah frequently dreams of flying over vast landscapes, feeling a sense of exhilaration and freedom as she soars through the clouds. She interprets these dreams as a reflection of her desire to break free from the constraints of her mundane existence and pursue her passions and aspirations with confidence and determination.

Falling:

Insecurity and Vulnerability: Dreams of falling often symbolize feelings of insecurity, vulnerability, or loss of control. The sensation of plummeting from great heights represents a fear of failure, rejection, or inadequacy in waking life.

Anxiety and Stress: Falling dreams may also reflect feelings of anxiety, stress, or pressure. The experience of free-falling without a safety net represents a sense of being overwhelmed by life's challenges and uncertainties.

Acceptance of Change: Falling dreams can also signify acceptance of change, transitions, or letting go of the past. The sensation of surrendering to gravity represents a willingness to embrace the unknown and trust in the process of change and transformation.

Example: Alex often dreams of falling from a great height, experiencing a sense of panic and helplessness as he plummets towards the ground. He interprets these dreams as a reflection of his fear of failure and insecurity about his ability to succeed in his career and personal life.

Being Chased:

Fear and Anxiety: Dreams of being chased often symbolize feelings of fear, anxiety, or vulnerability. The pursuit by an unknown assailant represents a threat to one's safety, security, or sense of self in waking life.

Avoidance and Escapism: Chasing dreams may also reflect a desire to avoid or escape from a threatening situation or confrontation. The sensation of being pursued relentlessly represents a fear of facing difficult emotions or unresolved conflicts.

Persistence of Unresolved Issues: Being chased dreams can also signify the persistence of unresolved issues or conflicts that need to be addressed. The recurring nature of these dreams may indicate a need to confront and resolve underlying fears or anxieties.

Example: Maya frequently dreams of being chased by a shadowy figure, experiencing a sense of terror and desperation as she tries to outrun her pursuer. She interprets these dreams as a reflection of her fear of confrontation and avoidance of difficult emotions or situations in waking life.

Nudity:

Vulnerability and Exposure: Dreams of nudity often symbolize feelings of vulnerability, exposure, or embarrassment. The sensation of being naked in public represents a fear of judgment, rejection, or social scrutiny.

Authenticity and Self-Acceptance: Nudity dreams may also reflect a desire for authenticity, transparency, or self-acceptance. The experience of being naked without shame or inhibition represents a longing to embrace one's true self and let go of pretense or social masks.

Sexuality and Intimacy: Nudity dreams can also carry sexual connotations, symbolizing issues related to sexuality, intimacy, or body image. The exposure of one's nakedness represents a desire for intimacy, connection, or acceptance of one's physicality.

Example: Jake frequently dreams of being naked in public, feeling a sense of shame and embarrassment as he tries to cover himself. He interprets these dreams as a reflection of his fear of being judged or rejected for his true self and his struggle to embrace his vulnerability and authenticity.

Teeth Falling Out:

Loss of Control and Powerlessness: Dreams of teeth falling out often symbolize feelings of loss of control, powerlessness, or insecurity. The sensation of losing one's teeth represents a fear of losing one's ability to communicate, assert oneself, or maintain a sense of identity.

Anxiety and Insecurity: Teeth falling out dreams may also reflect feelings of anxiety, insecurity, or self-doubt. The experience of losing one's teeth can evoke a sense of vulnerability, embarrassment, or inadequacy in waking life.

Transition and Renewal: Teeth falling out dreams can also signify transitions, changes, or renewal. The shedding of old teeth represents a process of letting go of the past and making way for new growth, opportunities, or experiences.

Example: Emily frequently dreams of her teeth falling out, experiencing a sense of panic and distress as she watches them crumble in her hands. She interprets these dreams as a reflection of her fear of losing control and her anxiety about her ability to assert herself and communicate effectively in her personal and professional life.

Being Lost or Trapped:

Fear and Confusion: Dreams of being lost or trapped often symbolize feelings of fear, confusion, or uncertainty. The sensation of being disoriented or confined represents a sense of being overwhelmed by life's challenges or unsure of one's direction.

Isolation and Alienation: Lost or trapped dreams may also reflect feelings of isolation, alienation, or loneliness. The experience of being separated from others or unable to find one's way home represents a fear of abandonment or disconnection.

Seeking Direction and Purpose: Being lost or trapped dreams can also signify a search for direction, purpose, or meaning. The struggle to navigate unfamiliar terrain or escape confinement represents a desire to find one's path or break free from limitations.

Example: Max often dreams of wandering through a maze-like labyrinth, feeling a sense of frustration and hopelessness as he searches for a way out. He interprets these dreams as a reflection of his uncertainty about his future and his struggle to find his place in the world.

Being Late or Missing an Important Event:

Anxiety and Stress: Dreams of being late or missing an important event often symbolize feelings of anxiety, stress, or pressure. The fear of being judged, criticized, or punished for one's tardiness represents a fear of failure or inadequacy.

Inadequacy and Self-Doubt: Being late dreams may also reflect feelings of inadequacy, self-doubt, or insecurity. The sensation of being unprepared or ill-equipped for the task at hand represents a fear of falling short of expectations or letting others down.

Regret and Missed Opportunities: Being late or missing an important event dreams can also signify regret or missed opportunities. The sense of disappointment or regret at missing out on a significant experience represents a longing to seize the moment and make the most of life's opportunities.

Example: Rachel frequently dreams of being late for her final exams, experiencing a sense of panic and dread as she rushes to the exam hall. She interprets these dreams as a reflection of her fear of failure and her anxiety about meeting others' expectations in her academic and professional pursuits.

Being Unable to Speak or Scream:

Helplessness and Frustration: Dreams of being unable to speak or scream often symbolize feelings of helplessness, frustration, or powerlessness. The sensation of being silenced or voiceless represents a fear of being ignored, invalidated, or unable to express oneself.

Fear and Anxiety: Being unable to speak dreams may also reflect feelings of fear, anxiety, or dread. The inability to vocalize one's distress or call for help represents a fear of being unheard or misunderstood in waking life.

Suppression and Self-Censorship: Dreams of being unable to speak or scream can also signify suppression or self-censorship. The experience of being silenced or muzzled represents a fear of speaking one's truth or asserting one's boundaries.

Example: Michael frequently dreams of trying to scream for help but finding no sound coming out of his mouth, feeling a sense of frustration and desperation as he struggles to make himself heard. He interprets these dreams as a reflection of his fear of being ignored or invalidated in his personal and professional relationships.

Being Attacked or Injured:

Fear and Vulnerability: Dreams of being attacked or injured often symbolize feelings of fear, vulnerability, or victimization. The sensation of being threatened or harmed by an assailant represents a fear of being targeted or victimized in waking life.

Conflict and Aggression: Being attacked dreams may also reflect feelings of anger, aggression, or conflict. The confrontation with an aggressor or assailant represents a struggle to defend oneself or assert one's boundaries in the face of opposition.

Healing and Resilience: Dreams of being attacked or injured can also signify healing and resilience. The experience of overcoming adversity or surviving an attack represents a triumph of the spirit and a reaffirmation of one's strength and resilience.

Example: David frequently dreams of being chased and attacked by shadowy figures, experiencing a sense of terror and helplessness as he tries to defend himself. He interprets these dreams as a reflection of his fear of being targeted or victimized in his personal and professional relationships, as well as his struggle to assert himself and defend his boundaries.

Death or Dying:

Change and Transformation: Dreams of death or dying often symbolize endings, transitions, or transformations. The experience of death represents a symbolic shedding of the old self and a rebirth into a new phase of life or existence.

Fear and Mortality: Death dreams may also reflect feelings of fear, anxiety, or mortality. The fear of death represents a primal instinct to preserve life and avoid the unknown or unknowable aspects of existence.

Closure and Acceptance: Dreams of death or dying can also signify closure, acceptance, or resolution. The experience of confronting one's mortality represents a willingness to let go of the past and embrace the present moment with gratitude and acceptance.

Example: Laura frequently dreams of witnessing her own death, experiencing a sense of peace and acceptance as she embraces the end of her life. She interprets these dreams as a reflection of her readiness to let go of old habits, beliefs, and attachments and embrace the unknown with courage and serenity.

Being Lost in a Crowd:

Alienation and Loneliness: Dreams of being lost in a crowd often symbolize feelings of alienation, loneliness, or disconnection from others. The sensation of being surrounded by people yet feeling invisible or insignificant represents a fear of being overlooked or misunderstood.

Identity and Self-Worth: Being lost in a crowd dreams may also reflect issues related to identity, self-worth, or belonging. The struggle to find one's place or assert one's individuality amidst the masses represents a search for validation, acceptance, or recognition.

Social Anxiety and Overwhelm: Dreams of being lost in a crowd can also signify social anxiety or overwhelm. The experience of navigating a sea of faces and voices without direction represents a fear of social judgment, rejection, or scrutiny.

Example: Ryan frequently dreams of wandering through a bustling city street, feeling a sense of isolation and insignificance amidst the throngs of people. He interprets these dreams as a reflection of his fear of being overlooked or dismissed by others in his personal and professional life.

Being Unprepared for an Exam or Presentation:

Fear of Failure and Judgment: Dreams of being unprepared for an exam or presentation often symbolize feelings of fear, inadequacy, or self-doubt. The fear of being judged, criticized, or exposed as incompetent represents a fear of failure or humiliation.

Pressure and Expectations: Being unprepared dreams may also reflect feelings of pressure, stress, or overwhelm. The sensation of scrambling to meet deadlines or expectations represents a fear of falling short of others' standards or not measuring up to one's own aspirations.

Self-Reflection and Evaluation: Dreams of being unprepared for an exam or presentation can also signify a need for self-reflection and evaluation. The experience of facing scrutiny or assessment represents a desire to evaluate one's progress, skills, or readiness for challenges.

Example: Emma frequently dreams of arriving late for an important exam, feeling a sense of panic and dread as she realizes she hasn't studied or prepared. She interprets these dreams as a reflection of her fear of failure and her anxiety about meeting others' expectations in her academic and professional pursuits.

Encountering a Deceased Loved One:

Grief and Loss: Dreams of encountering a deceased loved one often symbolize feelings of grief, longing, or unresolved emotions. The presence of the deceased represents a longing for connection, closure, or reconciliation with the past.

Closure and Healing: Encountering a deceased loved one in dreams can also signify a need for closure and healing. The opportunity to reconnect with the departed represents a chance to say goodbye, express love, or seek forgiveness.

Spiritual Connection and Guidance: Dreams of encountering a deceased loved one may also carry spiritual connotations, symbolizing a belief in an afterlife or spiritual realm. The presence of the departed may serve as a source of comfort, guidance, or reassurance in times of uncertainty or distress.

Example: Sarah frequently dreams of her deceased grandmother, feeling a sense of warmth and comfort as they share a conversation or embrace. She interprets these dreams as a reflection of her longing for her grandmother's guidance and wisdom, as well as her desire to feel connected to her spiritual roots.

Being Unable to Run or Move:

Powerlessness and Paralysis: Dreams of being unable to run or move often symbolize feelings of powerlessness, paralysis, or inertia. The sensation of being immobilized or trapped represents a fear of being unable to escape from threatening situations or confront challenges.

Fear and Vulnerability: Being unable to run dreams may also reflect feelings of fear, vulnerability, or helplessness. The experience of being unable to flee from danger or defend oneself represents a fear of being victimized or overwhelmed by life's challenges.

Inner Conflict and Resistance: Dreams of being unable to run or move can also signify inner conflict or resistance. The struggle to break free from constraints or barriers represents a desire to assert oneself, assert boundaries, or overcome obstacles.

Example: Mark frequently dreams of trying to run from an unseen threat but finding his legs rooted to the ground, feeling a sense of frustration and terror as he struggles to escape. He interprets these dreams as a reflection of his fear of being trapped or powerless in his personal and professional life.

Encountering a Monster or Demon:

Fear and Anxiety: Dreams of encountering a monster or demon often symbolize feelings of fear, anxiety, or dread. The presence of a malevolent entity represents a fear of danger, harm, or evil in waking life.

Shadow Self and Unconscious Fears: Encountering a monster or demon in dreams may also signify a confrontation with one's shadow self or unconscious fears. The monstrous figure represents aspects of the self that have been repressed, denied, or disowned.

Confronting Inner Demons: Dreams of encountering a monster or demon can also signify a need to confront inner demons or face unresolved issues. The battle with the creature represents a struggle to overcome obstacles, fears, or negative emotions.

Example: John frequently dreams of being pursued by a grotesque monster, feeling a sense of terror and despair as he tries to escape its clutches. He interprets these dreams as a reflection of his inner turmoil and his struggle to confront unresolved traumas or fears from his past.

These examples illustrate how common dream themes can provide valuable insights into the dreamer's emotions, thoughts, and experiences. While the interpretation of dreams is subjective and influenced by personal context, cultural beliefs, and individual experiences, exploring common dream themes can deepen our understanding of the human psyche and the mysteries of the unconscious mind. By paying attention to the recurring motifs, symbols, and emotions that appear in our dreams, we can gain valuable insights into our innermost thoughts, feelings, and desires, and unlock the hidden wisdom of the dreaming mind.

Understanding the psychological significance of common dream scenarios requires a nuanced exploration of the emotions, contexts, and personal associations embedded within each dream. Dreams act as mirrors reflecting the intricacies of the dreamer's inner world, inviting introspection and self-discovery.

Navigating the Dreamscapes of the Mind

In the vast landscapes of our dreams, we traverse symbolic terrains that resonate with the universal and the culturally specific. Common dream themes, imbued with psychological significance, offer glimpses into the labyrinthine recesses of the subconscious mind. As we navigate the dreamscapes of the mind, we unveil the interconnected layers of our shared humanity, cultural diversity, and individual psyches.

The exploration of universal dream symbols reveals the archetypal language spoken by the soul, transcending cultural boundaries and echoing the collective human experience. Yet, within this universality, cultural variations infuse dreams with diverse meanings, enriching the tapestry of interpretations and underscoring the importance of cultural sensitivity in dream analysis.

Psychological insights into common dream scenarios provide a roadmap for self-discovery, guiding the dreamer through the landscapes of emotion, desire, and unresolved conflicts. Dreams, like cryptic messages from the inner self, invite us to engage in a dialogue with the unconscious, unraveling the symbolic threads that weave the narratives of the night.

As we conclude this exploration of common dream themes, we carry with us the awareness that dreams are not mere ephemeral fragments of the night but intricate reflections of our conscious and subconscious minds. The dreamscapes we traverse hold the keys to self-understanding, offering a profound journey into the depths of the human psyche. In the realm of dreams, we continue to navigate, interpret, and decipher the mysteries that unfold beneath the starlit canopy of the unconscious mind.

Chapter 5

The Language of Dreams

In the nocturnal realm, where reality blurs and the subconscious takes the stage, dreams unfold as a complex tapestry of symbols, metaphors, and emotions. Deciphering the language of dreams is akin to unraveling a coded message from the inner self—a communication veiled in the enigmatic imagery of the unconscious mind. In this chapter, we embark on a journey into the intricate language of dreams, exploring the role of metaphor and symbolism, guiding you on how to recognize your personal symbols and their meanings, and delving into the emotional language woven into the fabric of your nocturnal narratives.

The Role of Metaphor and Symbolism in Dreams

Dreams speak a language distinct from the waking world, and their lexicon is one of symbols and metaphors. In this realm, everyday objects transform into potent symbols, and seemingly mundane scenarios unfold as allegorical tales. Understanding the role of metaphor and symbolism in dreams is essential for unlocking the rich layers of meaning embedded within the nocturnal narratives.

Metaphors as Bridges to the Unconscious: Metaphors serve as bridges that connect the conscious and unconscious realms. The mind, in its quest to convey complex emotions and experiences, often employs metaphors in dreams to communicate more profound truths. For example, a dream featuring a stormy sea might metaphorically represent the turbulence of the dreamer's emotions, allowing the unconscious to express what words may fail to convey in waking life.

Universal Symbols and Cultural Influences: While some symbols are universal, carrying archetypal meanings across cultures, others are culturally specific, drawing on individual and societal experiences. Universal symbols, such as the serpent or the labyrinth, tap into the collective unconscious, resonating with shared human experiences. Cultural symbols, on the other hand, may reflect personal associations and societal narratives that shape the dreamer's understanding of the world.

Objects as Symbols: Everyday objects take on symbolic significance in dreams, transcending their literal meanings. A key, for instance, might symbolize unlocking hidden potential or gaining access to new opportunities. Recognizing the symbolic resonance of objects in dreams invites the dreamer to explore the metaphorical dimensions of their waking life experiences.

Animals as Messengers: Animals often appear as powerful symbols in dreams, embodying archetypal qualities and instincts. The eagle might symbolize vision and perspective, while the serpent may represent transformation and renewal. The presence of animals in dreams invites a deeper exploration of primal instincts and symbolic meanings associated with each creature.

Settings and Landscapes: The landscapes and settings in dreams are not merely backdrops but hold symbolic significance. A dream set in a dense forest may represent the unexplored realms of the subconscious, while a vast desert might signify a feeling of isolation or emotional aridity. Examining the symbolic resonance of dreamscapes provides insights into the dreamer's inner landscape.

Recurring Symbols: Paying attention to recurring symbols in dreams unveils patterns that may carry specific messages. A recurring dream of a staircase, for instance, might signify a journey of personal growth or a desire to ascend to new heights. The persistence of certain symbols invites the dreamer to delve into the underlying themes and emotions associated with these recurring motifs.

Understanding the role of metaphor and symbolism in dreams requires a willingness to embrace the ambiguity and fluidity of the dream language. Symbols, like facets of a multifaceted gem, refract different meanings based on the dreamer's experiences, emotions, and the cultural context in which they are embedded.

How to Recognize Personal Symbols and Their Meanings

Just as a word might hold diverse meanings depending on the context, personal symbols in dreams carry nuanced significance shaped by the individual's experiences, memories, and emotions. Recognizing your personal symbols and understanding their meanings requires a process of introspection, self-awareness, and a willingness to explore the depths of your psyche.

Dream Journaling: Keeping a dream journal is a powerful tool for uncovering personal symbols. Regularly recording your dreams creates a repository of imagery and themes that recur over time. As you review your dream journal, patterns and symbols unique to your inner world may emerge, offering clues to the language your unconscious mind employs.

Reflecting on Emotional Resonance: Paying attention to the emotional tone of your dreams provides valuable insights into the significance of symbols. Note the feelings evoked by specific symbols or scenarios—whether it's a sense of joy, fear, nostalgia, or unease. Emotions act as signposts, guiding you toward the core meanings encoded within the dream symbolism.

Examining Life Associations: Personal symbols often draw from your waking life experiences and associations. Reflect on the symbolic resonance of objects, places, or individuals in your dreams and consider their relevance to your life story. A childhood home, for instance, may symbolize a longing for security or a desire to reconnect with aspects of your past.

Engaging in Symbolic Dialogue: Embark on a journey of symbolic dialogue by actively engaging with your dream symbols. Imaginatively explore the meanings and associations of specific symbols, allowing your intuition to guide you. Visualizations, artistic expressions, or conversations with these symbols in waking life can deepen your understanding of their personal significance.

Seeking Patterns in Recurring Dreams: Recurring dreams often feature consistent symbols that warrant attention. Whether it's a recurrent animal, object, or setting, these symbols may hold key messages from the subconscious. Analyze the patterns and variations within recurring dreams to unravel the layers of meaning encapsulated by these persistent symbols.

Consulting with Your Inner Guide: In the realm of dreams, your inner guide—the intuitive and wisdom-seeking aspect of your psyche—can play a crucial role in deciphering symbols. Before sleep, set an intention to receive guidance or insights related to your dreams. Trust the inner wisdom that emerges, and be open to the symbolic language that unfolds in response to your queries.

Recognizing personal symbols is a dynamic and evolving process. As you deepen your relationship with your dreams, you may discover new layers of symbolism and witness the fluidity of meanings that adapt to the changing landscape of your inner world.

Deciphering the Emotional Language in Dreams

Emotions are the raw, unfiltered expressions of the soul, and in the language of dreams, they form a nuanced and vivid palette. Deciphering the emotional language in dreams involves attuning to the subtle nuances of feelings that permeate the dreamscapes. Understanding the emotional landscape of dreams adds a layer of depth to the interpretation, offering insights into the dreamer's innermost desires, fears, and unresolved conflicts.

Identifying Primary Emotions: Begin by identifying the primary emotions experienced in a dream. Whether it's joy, fear, anger, sadness, or surprise, emotions serve as the emotional syntax through which the dream communicates. Acknowledge the dominant emotional tone of the dream as it provides a gateway to the underlying messages.

Exploring Mixed Emotions: Dreams often weave a tapestry of mixed emotions, creating a rich emotional landscape. Pay attention to the interplay of conflicting or contrasting emotions within the dream. For example, a dream featuring both fear and excitement may reflect the ambivalence or tension surrounding a particular waking life situation.

Examining Emotional Transitions: Dreams may unfold as emotional narratives, with shifts in mood and tone mirroring the twists and turns of the dreamer's inner journey. Observe how emotions transition from one scene to another, noting any significant shifts. These transitions may correspond to the dreamer's evolving attitudes, desires, or emotional responses in waking life.

Noting Repressed Emotions: Dreams provide a safe space for the expression of repressed or unacknowledged emotions. The subconscious mind, unrestricted by waking life constraints, may bring forth emotions that the conscious mind attempts to suppress. Recognizing and acknowledging these repressed emotions in dreams can contribute to emotional catharsis and self-discovery.

Analyzing Emotional Intensity: The intensity of emotions in dreams may serve as a gauge for the dreamer's emotional investment in specific themes or situations. A dream characterized by heightened emotions may highlight areas of significance or unresolved issues that demand attention. Analyze the emotional intensity as a cue for the dream's importance within the broader context of your inner world.

Connecting Dream Emotions to Waking Life: Draw connections between the emotions experienced in dreams and your waking life experiences. Consider whether the dream emotions reflect current circumstances, past memories, or unmet emotional needs. The emotional language of dreams often mirrors the dreamer's internal landscape, providing a window into the emotional terrain that shapes waking reality.

Using Dreams for Emotional Processing: Dreams act as a natural mechanism for emotional processing, helping the mind navigate and integrate complex feelings. Engage in reflective practices, such as journaling or artistic expression, to explore and process the emotions evoked by dreams. This intentional exploration contributes to emotional awareness and facilitates the integration of dream insights into waking life.

Understanding the emotional language of dreams requires attunement to the subtle nuances of feelings and an openness to exploring the depths of your emotional reservoir. As you navigate the dreamscapes, remember that emotions are not mere ephemeral sensations but potent messengers that convey the profound truths of the soul.

Unveiling the Secrets Within

In the realm of dreams, where metaphor, symbolism, and emotions converge, a language unfolds—a language that speaks to the core of our being. The symbols that dance across the nocturnal canvas are not mere random images but carriers of profound messages, reflections of our innermost desires, fears, and the landscapes of the soul.

As you venture into the language of dreams, consider yourself an ardent explorer navigating uncharted territories. Metaphors beckon, symbols whisper, and emotions resonate—a symphony of the subconscious seeking expression. The journey of unraveling this language is a process of self-discovery, a sacred dialogue with the depths of your psyche.

Embrace the ambiguity, savor the mysteries, and allow the language of dreams to guide you toward the unveiling of the secrets within. As you decipher the symbols, recognize personal motifs, and attune to the emotional resonances, you embark on a transformative journey—one that transcends the boundaries between the waking and dreaming self.

In the language of dreams, hidden truths become visible, and the veils of the subconscious are lifted. Trust the wisdom that emanates from the dreamscapes, for within their enigmatic narratives lie the keys to self-understanding, empowerment, and the endless exploration of the boundless realms within.

Chapter 6

Dreams as a Window to the Subconscious

In the labyrinthine corridors of the mind, dreams serve as illuminated windows, offering glimpses into the vast expanse of the subconscious. Within this realm, the subconscious mind weaves intricate narratives, unfurling symbolic landscapes that reflect our deepest desires, fears, and unresolved conflicts. In this chapter, we embark on a journey into the depths of the subconscious, exploring the ways in which dreams illuminate its mysteries, examining their connection to our waking life issues and stresses, and unveiling techniques for recalling and recording the treasures that lie within.

Understanding the Subconscious Mind through Dreams

The subconscious mind, like an underground river flowing beneath the surface of consciousness, holds the secrets of our innermost selves. While the conscious mind navigates the waking world, the subconscious orchestrates the symphony of our thoughts, emotions, and memories, shaping our perceptions and guiding our actions. Dreams serve as portals to this hidden realm, offering glimpses into its depths and providing avenues for self-discovery and exploration.

Symbolic Language of the Subconscious: The subconscious communicates through a symbolic language, rich in metaphor and imagery, weaving intricate narratives that speak to the depths of our being. In dreams, everyday objects transform into potent symbols, imbued with layers of meaning and significance. A simple house becomes a metaphor for the self, its rooms representing different aspects of our personality and inner world. Water symbolizes the ebb and flow of emotions, with calm seas signifying inner peace and turbulent waves reflecting emotional turmoil. Animals embody primal instincts and desires, while landscapes evoke the vast expanse of the unconscious mind.

By deciphering these symbols, we gain insight into the unconscious desires, fears, and conflicts that shape our waking reality. The appearance of a snake may signify hidden fears or repressed desires, while flying may represent a longing for freedom or escape. Dreams of falling may reflect feelings of insecurity or loss of control, while dreams of being chased may symbolize unresolved conflicts or anxieties. Each symbol holds a key to unlocking the mysteries of the subconscious mind, offering clues to the underlying dynamics of our psyche.

Through dream analysis and interpretation, we can uncover the hidden meanings of these symbols and integrate them into our conscious awareness. By engaging with the symbolic language of the subconscious, we embark on a journey of self-discovery and transformation, unraveling the mysteries of our innermost selves. As we delve deeper into the realm of dreams, we unlock the wisdom they offer, guiding us on the path to wholeness and fulfillment.

Processing Unconscious Material: Dreams act as the subconscious's playground, where repressed thoughts, emotions, and memories find expression. Through the symbolic narratives of dreams, the subconscious processes unresolved issues, confronts buried traumas, and integrates fragmented aspects of the self. Dream analysis provides a pathway for accessing and understanding this unconscious material, facilitating healing and personal growth.

Creative Source: The subconscious mind is a wellspring of creativity, birthing innovative ideas, artistic visions, and inspired insights. Dreams often serve as conduits for creative inspiration, offering glimpses of untapped potential and unexplored realms of imagination. By tapping into the creative reservoir of the subconscious, we harness its transformative power to fuel artistic endeavors and unlock new horizons of possibility.

Intuition and Gut Feelings: Intuition, often referred to as the subtle whisper of the soul, emanates from the depths of the subconscious mind, where it resides as a silent guide and guardian of our inner truth. Dreams serve as messengers of intuition, bridging the gap between the conscious and unconscious realms to impart guidance and wisdom that transcends rational thought. As we slumber, our minds drift into the mysterious landscape of dreams, where the language of symbolism speaks volumes and the wisdom of the subconscious unfolds.

By honing our ability to interpret dream symbolism and listen to the inner voice of intuition, we gain access to a profound source of inner knowing and insight. Dreams may offer subtle nudges in the right direction, signaling opportunities or warning of potential pitfalls. They may illuminate hidden truths or reveal aspects of ourselves that we have long overlooked or denied. Like a compass guiding us through the uncharted territory of our inner landscape, intuition speaks to us through the language of dreams, guiding us toward greater clarity, authenticity, and alignment with our deepest values and aspirations.

Through the practice of dreamwork and intuitive listening, we cultivate a deeper connection to our inner wisdom and intuition. We learn to trust the subtle signals and sensations that arise from within, recognizing them as valuable guideposts on our journey of self-discovery and growth. As we attune ourselves to the language of dreams and the whispers of intuition, we tap into a wellspring of insight and guidance that empowers us to navigate life's challenges with grace and clarity.

Dreams and Their Connection to Our Waking Life Issues and Stresses

The threads of our waking life experiences are woven into the fabric of our dreams, creating a tapestry of interconnected narratives that bridge the conscious and subconscious realms. Dreams serve as mirrors, reflecting the joys, challenges, and complexities of our everyday existence. By unraveling the threads of dream symbolism, we gain clarity and perspective on the issues and stresses that permeate our waking reality.

Emotional Processing: Dreams provide a safe space for emotional processing, allowing the subconscious to metabolize the highs and lows of daily life. Stressful events, unresolved conflicts, and unexpressed emotions often find expression in dreams, serving as a release valve for pent-up tension and anxiety. By acknowledging and exploring the emotions evoked by dreams, we engage in a process of emotional catharsis and self-healing.

Problem Solving and Insight: The subconscious mind is a formidable problem solver, capable of synthesizing information and generating innovative solutions. Dreams often offer insights and perspectives that elude the conscious mind, shedding light on complex issues and dilemmas. By incubating problems within the fertile soil of the subconscious, we tap into its creative potential and unlock fresh perspectives that lead to breakthroughs and resolutions.

Relationship Dynamics: Dreams serve as a window into the intricate dynamics of our relationships, offering a glimpse into the subconscious currents that shape our interactions with others. Within the realm of dreams, the complexities of human connection unfold in vivid detail, revealing the hidden truths and unspoken emotions that underlie our relationships. Conflicts, tensions, and unresolved issues often find expression in our dreams, presenting us with an opportunity for introspection and reconciliation.

Relationship-themed dreams may feature encounters with loved ones, friends, or acquaintances, each interaction laden with symbolic significance and emotional resonance. The emotions evoked in these dreams—whether love, anger, fear, or longing—reflect the underlying dynamics of our relationships and the unresolved feelings that linger beneath the surface. Through the exploration of dream symbolism and the analysis of recurring themes and motifs, we gain insight into the complexities of human connection and the underlying patterns that shape our relationships.

By delving into the symbolism and emotions embedded within relationship-themed dreams, we cultivate a deeper understanding of ourselves and others, fostering empathy, compassion, and mutual respect. Dreams provide a safe space for exploring the intricacies of our relationships, allowing us to confront unresolved issues, heal emotional wounds, and strengthen the bonds that connect us to one another. Through the process of dreamwork and reflection, we can navigate the complexities of human connection with greater clarity, insight, and grace, fostering harmonious and fulfilling relationships in our waking lives.

Physical Health and Well-Being: The mind-body connection is profoundly evident within the realm of dreams, where physical sensations often mirror our emotional and psychological states. In the mysterious landscape of the unconscious mind, dreams serve as a canvas upon which the body's innate wisdom is painted, offering insights into areas of imbalance or dis-ease. Physical sensations experienced in dreams—such as pain, discomfort, or vitality—can serve as powerful indicators of our overall health and well-being.

Dreams may reveal hidden tensions or unresolved emotions that manifest as physical symptoms in the waking world. For example, recurring dreams of falling may indicate feelings of instability or a lack of support in our lives, while dreams of being chased may reflect underlying anxieties or fears that are affecting our physical health. By paying attention to these physical sensations and symbols within our dreams, we can gain valuable insights into the root causes of our discomfort and take proactive steps toward healing and wholeness.

Through the practice of dreamwork and self-reflection, we can cultivate a deeper awareness of our holistic well-being, integrating the wisdom of our dreams into our daily lives. By exploring the physical sensations and symbols that arise in our dreams, we can uncover unconscious patterns and behaviors that may be impacting our health and vitality. With this awareness, we can make informed choices that support our physical, emotional, and spiritual well-being, fostering a harmonious balance between mind, body, and spirit. Ultimately, by honoring the messages of our dreams and tending to our physical health and well-being, we can embark on a journey toward greater vitality, resilience, and wholeness in all areas of our lives.

Techniques for Recalling and Recording Dreams

Recalling and recording dreams is a foundational practice for engaging with the subconscious realm and unlocking its treasures. By developing a consistent approach to dream recall and documentation, we strengthen our connection to the subconscious, enhance our ability to interpret dream symbolism, and glean valuable insights from the nocturnal landscapes of the mind.

Setting Intentions: Before sleep, set a clear intention to remember your dreams upon waking. Affirmations, visualizations, or simple statements of intent can prime the subconscious to prioritize dream recall and facilitate the retention of dream content. By consciously directing your focus towards remembering your dreams, you create a receptive mindset that increases the likelihood of recalling dream imagery upon awakening.

Dream Journaling: Keep a dream journal by your bedside to capture dreams upon waking. Upon opening your eyes in the morning, remain still and allow dream fragments to resurface. Record any images, emotions, or sensations that linger, trusting that the act of writing reinforces memory retention and encourages future dream recall. The act of journaling not only serves as a means of preserving dream content but also facilitates deeper reflection and analysis of dream symbolism.

Recording Dream Content: When recording dreams, focus on capturing the essential details while they are still fresh in your mind. Describe the setting, characters, emotions, and significant events with as much detail as possible, using sensory language to evoke the richness of the dream experience. By immersing yourself in the narrative of the dream and documenting it in vivid detail, you enhance your ability to recall and interpret dream imagery.

Reflecting on Dream Themes: Review your dream journal regularly to identify recurring themes, symbols, and patterns. Reflect on the connections between dreams and your waking life experiences, noting any correlations or insights that emerge. By discerning the underlying themes and messages encoded within dreams, you deepen your understanding of the subconscious currents that shape your reality. This reflective practice helps to uncover hidden patterns and insights that may not be immediately apparent upon first glance.

Dream Incubation: Prior to sleep, pose a specific question or intention to the subconscious, inviting guidance or insight related to a particular issue or area of interest. Trust that the subconscious will respond in its own time, weaving the answer into the tapestry of your dreams. Upon waking, record any dream content related to your incubated question or intention, recognizing the wisdom inherent in the subconscious's response. Dream incubation allows you to actively engage with the subconscious mind, directing its focus toward specific areas of inquiry or exploration and facilitating the manifestation of relevant dream imagery.

Creating a Dream Ritual: Establish a pre-sleep ritual that signals to the subconscious the importance of dream recall and exploration. Engage in calming activities such as meditation, visualization, or gentle movement to prepare the mind for sleep and invite a receptive state of consciousness. By honoring the sacred space of dreams, you cultivate a deeper connection to the subconscious and open yourself to its transformative guidance. Creating a dedicated space and time for dreamwork enhances your receptivity to dream imagery and fosters a sense of reverence for the mysteries of the unconscious.

Recalling and recording dreams is not merely an exercise in memory retention but a sacred practice of communion with the subconscious. By embracing the techniques outlined above, you embark on a journey of self-discovery, engaging with the mysteries of the nocturnal realm, and unlocking the profound wisdom that lies within.

Navigating the Depths of the Subconscious

As we conclude our exploration of dreams as a window to the subconscious, we are reminded of the profound interconnectedness between the conscious and unconscious realms. Dreams, like mirrors reflecting the soul, offer glimpses into the hidden recesses of our innermost selves, inviting us to embark on a journey of self-discovery and transformation.

In the labyrinth of the subconscious, symbols shimmer like constellations, emotions surge like ocean tides, and insights illuminate like guiding stars. By navigating these depths with curiosity, courage, and reverence, we unveil the secrets that lie within, embracing the fullness of our humanity and the boundless potential of the psyche.

As you continue to engage with your dreams as a sacred dialogue with the subconscious, remember that you are embarking on a journey of profound significance—one that transcends the confines of time and space, and leads to the infinite expanses of the soul. Trust in the wisdom of your dreams, honor the insights they offer, and embrace the transformative power of self-discovery that awaits within the depths of the subconscious.

Chapter 7

Nightmares and Disturbing Dreams

In the dark recesses of the night, amidst the whispers of shadows and the echoes of the subconscious, nightmares and disturbing dreams emerge like specters, unsettling the tranquility of sleep. These nocturnal visitors, laden with fear, anxiety, and unease, cast a shadow over the dreamer's inner landscape, leaving behind lingering traces of discomfort and disquiet. In this chapter, we confront the nature of nightmares, explore what they might signify, discuss strategies for coping with and interpreting them, and delve into the potential healing power concealed within these unsettling dreams.

The Nature of Nightmares and What They Might Signify

Nightmares, those harbingers of dread that intrude upon the sanctuary of sleep, possess a mysterious allure, drawing us into the labyrinthine depths of our fears and anxieties. These unsettling dreams, characterized by vivid imagery, intense emotions, and a sense of imminent threat, serve as reflections of the subconscious mind's darkest recesses. But what do nightmares signify, and why do they haunt our nocturnal reveries?

Manifestations of Anxiety and Fear: At their core, nightmares are manifestations of anxiety and fear, magnifying our deepest worries and insecurities. The scenarios that unfold within these unsettling dreams often mirror real-life stressors, unresolved traumas, or subconscious anxieties that lurk beneath the surface of consciousness. By confronting these fears in the safe confines of the dream world, the subconscious seeks to process and integrate the emotional residue of waking life experiences.

Symbolic Messages from the Subconscious: Nightmares speak a language of symbols and metaphors, weaving allegorical narratives that encode hidden truths and unspoken desires. The monstrous creatures, ominous landscapes, and perilous situations that populate these unsettling dreams serve as mirrors, reflecting the shadow aspects of the psyche and inviting introspection into the deeper layers of the unconscious mind.

Disruptions in Sleep Architecture: Nightmares often occur during the rapid eye movement (REM) stage of sleep, a period characterized by heightened brain activity and vivid dreaming. Disruptions in sleep architecture, such as sleep disturbances, irregular sleep patterns, or sleep disorders like post-traumatic stress disorder (PTSD), may increase the likelihood of experiencing nightmares. Understanding the relationship between sleep physiology and dream content sheds light on the underlying mechanisms that give rise to these unsettling nocturnal experiences.

Processing Trauma and Emotional Distress: For individuals grappling with trauma or emotional distress, nightmares may serve as a mechanism for processing and integrating difficult experiences. Trauma-related nightmares, in particular, may replay traumatic events or evoke intense emotions associated with past traumas, offering an opportunity for catharsis and emotional release. While distressing in the moment, these dreams may contribute to the healing process by fostering greater resilience and adaptive coping strategies.

Strategies for Coping with and Interpreting Nightmares

In the face of nightmares' chilling embrace, it is natural to seek refuge from their unsettling grip. Yet, by confronting these nocturnal phantoms with courage and resilience, we uncover hidden reservoirs of strength and resilience within ourselves. Employing strategies for coping with and interpreting nightmares empowers us to reclaim agency over our dreams and harness their transformative potential.

Establishing a Relaxing Bedtime Routine: Cultivating a calming bedtime routine promotes relaxation and tranquility, creating an optimal environment for restorative sleep. Engage in soothing activities such as reading, gentle stretching, or mindfulness meditation to ease the transition from wakefulness to sleep. By fostering a sense of serenity before bedtime, you mitigate the likelihood of experiencing nightmares and promote restful sleep.

Creating a Safe Sleep Environment: Ensure that your sleep environment is conducive to relaxation and comfort, free from distractions or stimuli that may trigger anxiety or arousal. Dim the lights, minimize noise disruptions, and create a comfortable sleep space that invites a sense of security and safety. By establishing a sanctuary for sleep, you create a protective barrier against the intrusion of nightmares into your nocturnal realm.

Utilizing Imagery Rehearsal Therapy: Imagery rehearsal therapy (IRT) is a cognitive-behavioral technique that involves rewriting the script of nightmares to promote more positive outcomes. Engage in visualization exercises during waking hours, rehearsing alternative endings to recurring nightmares or transforming threatening dream imagery into symbols of empowerment and resilience. By reframing the narrative of nightmares through visualization and mental rehearsal, you reclaim control over the dream landscape and diminish their disruptive impact on sleep.

Exploring Dream Symbols and Themes: Nightmares, like all dreams, are laden with symbolic imagery that carries deeper meaning and significance. Engage in dream journaling to record and analyze the themes, symbols, and emotions that emerge within nightmares. By deciphering the symbolic language of dreams, you uncover the hidden messages encoded within nightmares, gaining insight into underlying fears, conflicts, and unresolved issues that demand attention and exploration.

Seeking Support from Mental Health Professionals: If nightmares persistently disrupt sleep or cause significant distress, consider seeking support from mental health professionals trained in dream work and trauma-informed care. Therapeutic interventions such as cognitive-behavioral therapy (CBT) for insomnia, exposure therapy, or eye movement desensitization and reprocessing (EMDR) may help alleviate nightmares and address underlying trauma or anxiety disorders. Collaborate with a qualified therapist to develop personalized coping strategies and therapeutic interventions tailored to your unique needs and circumstances.

The Potential Healing Power of Disturbing Dreams

Despite their unsettling nature, nightmares and disturbing dreams possess a hidden potential for healing and transformation. Beneath the veneer of fear and anxiety, these unsettling nocturnal visitors harbor profound insights, offering a pathway to self-discovery, emotional catharsis, and psychological resilience.

Catharsis and Emotional Release: Nightmares provide a cathartic outlet for processing intense emotions and releasing pent-up tension and anxiety. By confronting fears and anxieties within the safe confines of the dream world, the subconscious facilitates emotional release, allowing the dreamer to confront and integrate difficult experiences without fear of judgment or reprisal.

Integration of Traumatic Experiences: For individuals grappling with trauma or post-traumatic stress disorder (PTSD), nightmares may serve as a mechanism for processing and integrating traumatic experiences. Trauma-related nightmares may replay distressing events or evoke intense emotions associated with past traumas, fostering greater resilience and adaptive coping strategies over time. Through the process of exposure and desensitization, nightmares contribute to the gradual integration and resolution of traumatic memories, paving the way for healing and recovery.

Insights into Unconscious Dynamics: Nightmares offer a window into the deeper recesses of the unconscious mind, illuminating hidden fears, conflicts, and unresolved issues that shape waking life experiences. By exploring the themes, symbols, and emotions embedded within nightmares, the dreamer gains insight into the underlying dynamics that contribute to psychological distress and maladaptive patterns of behavior. This heightened self-awareness fosters personal growth and empowers the dreamer to confront and transform unconscious obstacles that inhibit their well-being and fulfillment.

Catalysts for Positive Change: Nightmares, when approached with courage and resilience, serve as catalysts for positive change and transformation. By confronting fears and anxieties within the dream landscape, the dreamer cultivates inner strength, resilience, and adaptive coping strategies that transcend the boundaries of sleep. Nightmares challenge the dreamer to confront adversity with courage and resilience, fostering personal growth, and empowerment in the face of life's challenges.

In the crucible of nightmares and disturbing dreams, we confront the shadows that dwell within the recesses of our subconscious, embracing their transformative potential and reclaiming agency over our inner landscape. By engaging with these unsettling nocturnal visitors with courage, compassion, and curiosity, we unearth hidden reservoirs of strength, resilience, and wisdom that illuminate the path toward healing, self-discovery, and psychological integration.

Embracing the Transformative Power of Nightmares

As we conclude our exploration of nightmares and disturbing dreams, we are reminded of their paradoxical nature—unsettling yet illuminating, frightening yet transformative. These nocturnal phantoms, laden with fear and anxiety, serve as gatekeepers to the hidden realms of the subconscious, offering profound insights and opportunities for growth amidst the shadows.

In the darkness of the night, where nightmares hold sway, we confront the depths of our fears and insecurities, engaging with the shadows that lurk within the recesses of our psyche. Through courage, resilience, and self-awareness, we navigate the labyrinthine landscapes of the dream world, unraveling the mysteries that lie within and harnessing their transformative potential for healing and self-discovery.

Embrace the shadows, confront the fears, and awaken to the transformative power concealed within the depths of nightmares and disturbing dreams. In the crucible of darkness, we discover the seeds of resilience, wisdom, and empowerment that flourish amidst the shadows, guiding us on the journey toward wholeness, integration, and self-empowerment.

Chapter 8

Lucid Dreaming

Taking Control of the Dream World

In the ethereal realm of dreams, where the boundaries between imagination and reality blur, lucid dreaming beckons as a gateway to boundless possibility and untapped potential. Lucid dreaming, the art of becoming aware within the dream state and exerting conscious control over the dream narrative, offers a transformative journey into the depths of the subconscious. In this chapter, we embark on an exploration of lucid dreaming, delving into its benefits, unveiling techniques for inducing lucid dreams, and elucidating how to harness the power of lucidity for self-discovery and problem-solving.

An Introduction to Lucid Dreaming and Its Benefits

Lucid dreaming, characterized by the awareness of being within a dream while it unfolds, represents a profound shift in consciousness—a liberation from the confines of passive observation to active participation in the dream landscape. Within the realm of lucid dreaming, dreamers wield the power to shape reality, manifest their desires, and explore the boundless horizons of the imagination. But beyond its inherent allure, lucid dreaming offers a host of benefits that extend into the realms of personal growth, creativity, and self-discovery.

Enhanced Creativity and Imagination: Lucid dreaming serves as a fertile playground for creativity and imagination, providing a canvas upon which dreamers can unleash their artistic visions and explore new realms of possibility. In the lucid dream state, the constraints of physical reality dissolve, opening the floodgates to infinite creative potential and innovative thinking. By harnessing the boundless expanses of the dream world, dreamers tap into a wellspring of inspiration and insight that transcends the limitations of waking life.

Overcoming Fears and Phobias: Lucid dreaming offers a safe environment for confronting and overcoming fears and phobias that may inhibit personal growth and well-being. By entering into dialogue with the subconscious mind within the lucid dream state, dreamers confront the sources of their fears, gaining insight and perspective that empowers them to transcend limiting beliefs and emotional obstacles. Through repeated exposure and desensitization within the controlled environment of the dream world, fears lose their grip, paving the way for greater courage, resilience, and self-assurance in waking life.

Enhanced Problem-Solving and Decision-Making: Lucid dreaming facilitates problem-solving and decision-making by providing a platform for experimentation, exploration, and creative insight. In the lucid dream state, dreamers have the freedom to test hypotheses, explore alternative scenarios, and visualize solutions to real-life challenges. By engaging in mental rehearsal and visualization within the dream landscape, dreamers prime their minds for success, enhancing cognitive flexibility, and adaptive problem-solving skills that translate into waking life endeavors.

Emotional Healing and Self-Integration: Lucid dreaming offers a pathway for emotional healing and self-integration by providing access to the deeper layers of the psyche and facilitating dialogue with the subconscious mind. Within the lucid dream state, dreamers confront unresolved emotional wounds, process traumatic experiences, and integrate fragmented aspects of the self. By engaging in symbolic dialogue and inner exploration within the safe confines of the dream world, dreamers foster greater self-awareness, acceptance, and emotional resilience that contribute to holistic well-being and personal fulfillment.

Spiritual Awakening and Transcendence: Lucid dreaming serves as a catalyst for spiritual awakening and transcendence, offering a direct experience of the interconnectedness of mind, body, and spirit. In the lucid dream state, dreamers tap into higher states of consciousness, accessing wisdom and insight that transcends the limitations of the egoic mind. By cultivating mindfulness, presence, and intentionality within the dream landscape, dreamers deepen their spiritual practice, forging a deeper connection to the divine and experiencing profound states of unity, bliss, and transcendence.

Techniques for Inducing Lucid Dreams

Embarking on the journey of lucid dreaming requires dedication, practice, and a willingness to explore the depths of consciousness. Fortunately, a myriad of techniques and practices exist to facilitate the induction of lucid dreams, empowering dreamers to unlock the gates of lucidity and embark on transformative journeys within the dream world.

Reality Testing: Reality testing involves regularly questioning the nature of reality and conducting reality checks throughout the day. By habitually questioning whether one is dreaming or awake, dreamers increase the likelihood of becoming lucid within the dream state. Common reality checks include attempting to read text, looking at one's hands, or attempting to pass through solid objects. By cultivating a habit of reality testing, dreamers develop greater self-awareness and discernment, leading to increased lucidity within dreams.

Mindfulness Meditation: Mindfulness meditation serves as a foundation for lucid dreaming practice, cultivating present-moment awareness and sharpening the faculty of introspection. By engaging in daily meditation practices, dreamers develop greater mindfulness, concentration, and self-awareness, creating fertile ground for lucid dreaming to take root. Mindfulness meditation also enhances dream recall and self-reflective awareness, facilitating the recognition of dream signs and the induction of lucid dreams.

Wake-Induced Lucid Dreaming (WILD): Wake-induced lucid dreaming (WILD) involves transitioning directly from waking consciousness into the lucid dream state while maintaining awareness throughout the process. To induce a WILD, dreamers lie still in a comfortable position as they enter the hypnagogic state—the transitional phase between wakefulness and sleep. By maintaining mental focus and awareness as the body falls asleep, dreamers enter directly into the lucid dream state, bypassing the typical transition from waking to dreaming consciousness.

Mnemonic Induction of Lucid Dreams (MILD): Mnemonic induction of lucid dreams (MILD) involves setting intentions to become lucid within dreams and using mnemonic cues to reinforce lucidity. Before sleep, dreamers affirm their intention to become lucid within dreams and visualize themselves recognizing dream signs and becoming aware within the dream state. Throughout the day, dreamers engage in reality testing and repeat affirmations to reinforce the intention to become lucid while dreaming. By integrating mnemonic cues and affirmations into daily routines, dreamers increase the likelihood of achieving lucidity within dreams.

Wake-Back-to-Bed (WBTB) Technique: The wake-back-to-bed (WBTB) technique involves waking up during the night, remaining awake for a brief period, and then returning to sleep with the intention of inducing lucid dreams. Upon waking, dreamers engage in reality testing, journaling dream content, or engaging in visualization exercises to reinforce the intention to become lucid within dreams. By interrupting the sleep cycle and re-entering REM sleep with heightened awareness, dreamers increase the likelihood of experiencing lucid dreams during subsequent sleep cycles.

Lucid Dreaming Supplements and Aids: Certain supplements and aids may enhance the induction of lucid dreams by promoting relaxation, enhancing dream recall, and facilitating cognitive clarity. Supplements such as galantamine, choline, and vitamin B6 have been reported to increase the frequency and intensity of lucid dreams when taken before bedtime. Additionally, lucid dreaming aids such as lucid dreaming masks, soundscapes, and guided meditations provide sensory cues and reminders to reinforce lucidity within dreams.

How to Use Lucid Dreaming for Self-Discovery and Problem-Solving

Lucid dreaming serves as a potent tool for self-discovery, problem-solving, and personal growth, offering a gateway to the hidden realms of the subconscious mind. By harnessing the power of lucidity, dreamers unlock the secrets of the psyche, gain insight into unconscious dynamics, and cultivate greater self-awareness and empowerment. Here are some strategies for using lucid dreaming for self-discovery and problem-solving:

Exploring Inner Landscapes: Within the lucid dream state, dreamers have the freedom to explore the landscapes of the subconscious mind, delving into the depths of the psyche and confronting hidden fears, desires, and unresolved conflicts. By engaging in symbolic dialogue with dream characters, exploring dream environments, and uncovering the meaning behind dream symbolism, dreamers gain insight into the underlying dynamics that shape their thoughts, emotions, and behaviors in waking life.

Confronting Fears and Limiting Beliefs: Lucid dreaming provides a safe environment for confronting fears, phobias, and limiting beliefs that may inhibit personal growth and well-being. By intentionally manifesting challenging scenarios within lucid dreams and confronting them with courage and resilience, dreamers diminish the power of fear and expand their comfort zones. Through repeated exposure and desensitization within the controlled environment of the dream world, dreamers cultivate greater emotional resilience and self-assurance that translates into waking life endeavors.

Visualizing Success and Achievement: Lucid dreaming serves as a powerful platform for mental rehearsal and visualization, allowing dreamers to practice skills, rehearse presentations, and visualize success in various areas of life. By entering into a lucid dream state with a specific goal or intention in mind, dreamers engage in visualization exercises that reinforce positive outcomes and foster a sense of confidence and mastery. Whether preparing for a performance, envisioning career success, or cultivating healthy habits, lucid dreaming provides a potent tool for manifesting desired outcomes and realizing one's full potential.

Seeking Guidance and Insight: Within the lucid dream state, dreamers may seek guidance and insight from higher wisdom sources, inner guides, or archetypal symbols that offer wisdom and perspective on life's challenges. By engaging in dialogue with dream characters, posing questions to the subconscious mind, or seeking guidance from dream guides and mentors, dreamers gain access to intuitive insights and creative solutions that transcend the limitations of rational thought. Through the practice of dream incubation and intention setting, dreamers invite transformative experiences and profound revelations that illuminate the path toward self-discovery and personal growth.

Problem-Solving and Creative Insight: Lucid dreaming facilitates problem-solving and creative insight by providing a platform for experimentation, exploration, and imaginative thinking. Within the lucid dream state, dreamers may pose specific questions or challenges to the subconscious mind, seeking creative solutions and innovative ideas that transcend conventional thinking. By engaging in visualizations, mental simulations, and thought experiments within the dream landscape, dreamers unlock novel perspectives and ingenious solutions to real-life challenges. Through the process of dream-inspired creativity and problem-solving, dreamers harness the transformative power of lucidity to overcome obstacles, seize opportunities, and realize their aspirations.

Embracing the Boundless Horizons of Lucid Dreaming

As we conclude our exploration of lucid dreaming, we are reminded of its transformative potential to awaken, empower, and inspire. Within the vast expanse of the dream world, lucidity beckons as a guiding light, illuminating the path toward self-discovery, creativity, and personal growth. By embracing the practices and principles of lucid dreaming, dreamers embark on a journey of boundless possibility and infinite potential—a journey that transcends the confines of time and space and leads to the discovery of the true self.

In the tapestry of consciousness, where dreams and waking life intersect, lucid dreaming serves as a bridge between the realms of imagination and reality. By cultivating awareness, intentionality, and presence within the dream landscape, dreamers reclaim agency over their inner world, manifest their desires, and embark on transformative journeys of self-discovery and empowerment. As you embark on your own journey of lucid dreaming, remember that the power to awaken lies within you—within the depths of your imagination, the expanses of your consciousness, and the limitless horizons of your dreams. Embrace the boundless horizons of lucid dreaming, and let the journey unfold.

Chapter 9

Dreams and Creativity

In the vast realm of the subconscious, where the imagination roams free and the boundaries of reality blur, dreams emerge as fertile grounds for creativity to flourish. Across cultures and throughout history, dreams have served as wellsprings of inspiration, birthing innovative ideas, artistic masterpieces, and revolutionary breakthroughs. In this chapter, we explore the symbiotic relationship between dreams and creativity, examining famous examples of dreams inspiring creative endeavors, elucidating how to harness dreams for artistic inspiration, and offering exercises for incubating creative dreams.

Famous Examples of Dreams Inspiring Creativity

Throughout the annals of history, countless visionaries, artists, and innovators have drawn inspiration from the wellspring of the subconscious, channeling the imagery, symbolism, and insights of dreams into works of art, literature, music, and scientific discovery. From ancient civilizations to modern-day luminaries, dreams have played a pivotal role in shaping the course of human creativity and innovation. Here are a few notable examples:

The Discovery of the Periodic Table: In 1869, Russian chemist Dmitri Mendeleev famously credited a dream with inspiring his groundbreaking discovery of the periodic table of elements. Legend has it that Mendeleev dreamed of arranging the elements in a systematic manner, with similar properties grouped together. Upon awakening, he hastily scribbled down his vision, laying the foundation for one of the most significant achievements in the history of chemistry.

Frankenstein: Mary Shelley's Dream of Creation: In 1816, Mary Shelley famously conceived the idea for her Gothic masterpiece "Frankenstein" in a dream. As the story goes, Shelley dreamt of a scientist who animated a creature from lifeless matter, sparking a chain of events that would forever alter the landscape of literature. Inspired by her dream, Shelley penned the iconic tale of Dr. Victor Frankenstein and his monstrous creation, exploring themes of ambition, hubris, and the consequences of playing god.

The Beatles' "Yesterday": Paul McCartney's Dream Composition: In 1965, Paul McCartney awoke from a vivid dream with the melody of "Yesterday" fully formed in his mind. Believing the tune to be an existing song, McCartney rushed to his piano to play the melody, only to realize it was a creation of his own subconscious. The hauntingly beautiful ballad would go on to become one of The Beatles' most beloved and enduring hits, showcasing the transformative power of dream-inspired creativity.

Salvador Dalí's Surrealist Masterpieces: Surrealist artist Salvador Dalí drew inspiration from the surreal landscapes and fantastical imagery of his dreams, incorporating dream symbolism and subconscious motifs into his iconic paintings. Dalí famously utilized the technique of "paranoiac-critical method," harnessing the power of his dreams to access deeper layers of creativity and imagination. Through his dream-inspired masterpieces such as "The Persistence of Memory" and "Dream Caused by the Flight of a Bee Around a Pomegranate a Second Before Awakening," Dalí forged a new artistic language that transcended the boundaries of reality and logic.

Kubla Khan: Coleridge's Dream of Xanadu: In 1797, Samuel Taylor Coleridge famously penned the visionary poem "Kubla Khan" after experiencing a vivid dream of the mythical palace of Xanadu. According to Coleridge's account, he fell into a deep slumber while reading a book about the Mongol emperor Kubla Khan and awoke with the poem fully formed in his mind. Despite being interrupted by a visitor before he could complete the poem, "Kubla Khan" remains a testament to the power of dreams to ignite the creative imagination.

Robert Louis Stevenson's "Dr. Jekyll and Mr. Hyde": The concept for Robert Louis Stevenson's novella "Strange Case of Dr. Jekyll and Mr. Hyde" reportedly emerged from a dream. Stevenson described the dream as a "fine bogey tale" that unfolded in his mind one night. The story explores the duality of human nature and the struggle between good and evil, reflecting Stevenson's subconscious exploration during sleep.

August Kekulé's Discovery of the Benzene Ring: The German chemist August Kekulé famously attributed his discovery of the benzene ring structure to a dream he had in 1865. Kekulé reportedly dreamt of a group of snakes biting their own tails, which inspired his insight into the cyclic structure of benzene. This dream revelation revolutionized organic chemistry and laid the groundwork for modern chemical theory.

James Cameron's "Terminator": Director James Cameron's blockbuster film "The Terminator" originated from a nightmare he had while working on a film in Rome. Cameron dreamt of a metallic torso emerging from an explosion, relentlessly pursuing him. This nightmare served as the genesis for the iconic character of the Terminator, a relentless cyborg assassin, and spawned a franchise that continues to captivate audiences worldwide.

The Invention of the Sewing Machine by Elias Howe: Elias Howe, the inventor of the sewing machine, reportedly had a breakthrough moment in a dream. In his dream, he found himself surrounded by cannibals who brandished spears with holes in the tips. This image inspired Howe's design for the needle with the eye at the pointed end, revolutionizing the textile industry and modernizing garment production.

Stephen King's "Misery": Stephen King's novel "Misery" was inspired by a nightmare he had during a stay at a secluded hotel. King dreamt of being held captive by a deranged fan who demanded he rewrite a novel to her liking. This chilling dream served as the foundation for the gripping tale of a bestselling author held captive by his psychotic number-one fan, showcasing King's ability to transform nightmares into compelling narratives.

The Discovery of the Double Helix Structure of DNA: The Nobel Prize-winning discovery of the double helix structure of DNA by James Watson and Francis Crick was reportedly influenced by a dream. According to Watson, he dreamt of two intertwined serpents that formed a double helix pattern, providing him with a visual representation of the DNA molecule's structure. This dream-inspired insight revolutionized genetics and molecular biology.

Richard Wagner's "Die Meistersinger von Nürnberg": German composer Richard Wagner claimed that the idea for his opera "Die Meistersinger von Nürnberg" came to him in a dream. Wagner recounted that he dreamt of a colossal musical contest taking place in medieval Nuremberg, which served as the basis for the opera's plot. This dream-inspired work became one of Wagner's most beloved operas, showcasing his mastery of music and storytelling.

J.K. Rowling's "Harry Potter" Series: Author J.K. Rowling famously revealed that the idea for the "Harry Potter" series came to her during a train journey. While traveling on a delayed train from Manchester to London, Rowling found herself daydreaming about a young boy attending a school for wizards. This initial spark of inspiration evolved into the magical world of Hogwarts and the beloved characters of Harry Potter, Ron Weasley, and Hermione Granger.

Keith Richards' Guitar Riff for "(I Can't Get No) Satisfaction": Rolling Stones guitarist Keith Richards famously claimed that the iconic guitar riff for "(I Can't Get No) Satisfaction" came to him in a dream. Richards woke up one morning with the riff fully formed in his mind and immediately recorded it on a cassette player before falling back asleep. This dream-inspired riff became one of the most recognizable and influential guitar lines in rock music history.

Frank Capra's "It's a Wonderful Life": Director Frank Capra's classic film "It's a Wonderful Life" was based on a short story titled "The Greatest Gift" by Philip Van Doren Stern. Stern reportedly wrote the story after experiencing a vivid dream in which he saw his own death and its impact on the lives of those around him. This dream-inspired tale of redemption and the power of human connection became a beloved holiday classic.

Dream Theater's Concept Album "Metropolis Pt. 2: Scenes from a Memory":

The progressive metal band Dream Theater created their concept album "Metropolis Pt. 2: Scenes from a Memory" based on a recurring dream experienced by drummer Mike Portnoy. Portnoy's dream served as the inspiration for the album's narrative, which follows the story of a man who experiences past-life regression therapy and uncovers a tragic love story set in the early 20th century.

Giuseppe Tartini's "Devil's Trill Sonata": Italian composer and violinist Giuseppe Tartini claimed that his famous "Devil's Trill Sonata" was inspired by a dream. In the dream, Tartini allegedly made a pact with the devil, who played a hauntingly beautiful violin sonata. Upon awakening, Tartini attempted to recreate the melody he heard in his dream, resulting in the composition of the virtuosic and expressive sonata.

Stephenie Meyer's "Twilight": Author Stephenie Meyer famously conceived the idea for her "Twilight" series through a dream. Meyer dreamt of a human girl and a vampire boy having a conversation in a meadow, which served as the spark for the love story between Bella Swan and Edward Cullen. This dream-inspired tale of forbidden love became a cultural phenomenon, captivating readers worldwide.

Albert Einstein's Theory of Relativity: While not directly attributed to a dream, Albert Einstein's theory of relativity is said to have been influenced by his thought experiments, which he described as akin to dreaming with one's eyes open. Einstein's revolutionary theories, including the theory of special and general relativity, transformed our understanding of space, time, and the universe, demonstrating the power of imaginative thinking and conceptual breakthroughs.

These examples offer a glimpse into the transformative power of dreams to inspire innovation, creativity, and artistic expression. From scientific breakthroughs to literary masterpieces, dreams continue to serve as a wellspring of inspiration for those willing to explore the depths of the subconscious and harness the creative potential that lies within.

How to Harness Dreams for Creative Endeavors

Harnessing the creative potential of dreams requires intentionality, receptivity, and a willingness to explore the depths of the subconscious. By cultivating practices and techniques that facilitate dream recall, interpretation, and integration, dreamers can unlock the hidden reservoirs of inspiration and insight that reside within the dream landscape. Here are some strategies for harnessing dreams for creative endeavors:

Dream Journaling: Keeping a dream journal is a foundational practice for harnessing dreams for creative inspiration. Upon waking, record any dreams, images, or emotions that linger in your mind, capturing the essence of the dream experience in written or visual form. By documenting dream content regularly, you strengthen your connection to the subconscious, enhance dream recall, and cultivate a repository of symbolic imagery and inspiration for creative exploration.

Dream Incubation: Dream incubation involves setting intentions before sleep to dream about specific topics, questions, or creative projects. By focusing your attention and intentionality on a particular theme or inquiry, you prime the subconscious to prioritize dream content related to your creative endeavors. Before bedtime, meditate on your creative goals, visualize the desired outcome, and affirm your intention to receive guidance and inspiration through your dreams. Trust that the subconscious will respond to your intentions and provide insights that fuel your creative process.

Visualizations and Guided Imagery: Engaging in visualizations and guided imagery exercises before sleep can enhance creative inspiration and facilitate dream incubation. Spend time visualizing yourself engaged in your creative pursuits, imagining the sights, sounds, and sensations associated with your desired outcomes. Create a mental blueprint of your creative vision, infusing it with energy, intention, and emotion. By immersing yourself in the creative process through visualization, you activate the subconscious mind and invite dream imagery that aligns with your intentions.

Active Imagination: Active imagination involves entering into dialogue with dream imagery and symbols through creative expression, such as writing, drawing, or role-playing. Engage with dream characters, symbols, and scenarios as if they were living entities, allowing them to communicate their insights and wisdom to you. Write dialogues with dream characters, create visual representations of dream scenes, or embody dream symbolism through movement and gesture. By actively engaging with dream imagery, you deepen your connection to the subconscious and access the creative insights and inspiration that reside within.

Mindfulness and Presence: Cultivating mindfulness and presence throughout the day fosters receptivity to creative inspiration and insight from the dream landscape. Practice mindfulness techniques such as meditation, breathwork, or sensory awareness to anchor yourself in the present moment and quiet the chatter of the mind. By cultivating a state of relaxed attentiveness and receptivity, you create fertile ground for creative ideas to emerge and integrate into your consciousness. Allow yourself to remain open and receptive to inspiration from unexpected sources, trusting that creative insights may arise spontaneously during waking life as well as within the dream state.

Exercises for Incubating Creative Dreams

In addition to the practices outlined above, specific exercises can be employed to incubate creative dreams and amplify the flow of inspiration and insight from the subconscious. Here are some exercises for incubating creative dreams:

Creative Visualization: Before bedtime, engage in a creative visualization exercise in which you imagine yourself immersed in your creative project or endeavor. Visualize the details of your creative vision, including the sights, sounds, and sensations associated with achieving your desired outcome. Allow yourself to embody the emotions of success, fulfillment, and creative expression as you visualize your goals coming to fruition.

Dream Affirmations: Create affirmations or mantras related to your creative aspirations and repeat them before sleep to program your subconscious mind for dream inspiration. Phrase affirmations in the present tense and with positive language, such as "I am a channel for creative inspiration," "My dreams are filled with innovative ideas," or

"I effortlessly tap into my creative genius while I sleep." Repeat these affirmations with conviction and intentionality, trusting that your subconscious will respond to your suggestions and provide creative insights through your dreams.

Creative Prompting: Pose specific questions or prompts related to your creative projects or areas of interest before sleep to stimulate dream content that addresses your inquiries. Write down questions such as "What is the next step in my creative process?" "How can I overcome creative blocks or challenges?" or "What innovative ideas are waiting to be discovered within my subconscious?" Allow these questions to percolate in your mind as you drift off to sleep, trusting that your dreams will provide answers and insights that propel your creative endeavors forward.

Dream Incubation Rituals: Create a bedtime ritual or ceremony that signifies your intention to receive creative inspiration through your dreams. Light candles, burn incense, or engage in relaxation techniques to signal to your subconscious mind that it is time to focus on your creative aspirations. Set an intention for the night's dreams, whether it be to receive guidance, insight, or inspiration related to your creative projects. By imbuing your bedtime routine with intentionality and symbolism, you create a sacred space for creative incubation and dream exploration.

Dreamscape Exploration: Explore dreamscapes related to your creative interests or artistic passions within the lucid dream state. As you become lucid within a dream, consciously direct your attention toward creative environments, settings, or scenarios that resonate with your creative vision. Engage with dream characters, symbols, and landscapes as if they were living embodiments of your creative muse, allowing them to guide you through the realms of imagination and inspiration. By immersing yourself in dreamscapes aligned with your creative aspirations, you access a limitless reservoir of artistic potential and visionary insight.

By incorporating these practices and exercises into your daily routine, you cultivate receptivity to creative inspiration and enhance the flow of insights and ideas from the subconscious. Trust in the creative wisdom that resides within you, and let your dreams serve as a guiding light on your journey of artistic expression and self-discovery.

Awakening the Creative Genius Within

As we conclude our exploration of dreams and creativity, we are reminded of the profound symbiosis between the realms of imagination and inspiration. Within the depths of the subconscious, where dreams dwell and creativity blossoms, lies a treasure trove of untapped potential waiting to be unearthed. By cultivating practices that honor the creative genius within, we unlock the gates of inspiration and embark on transformative journeys of self-discovery and artistic expression.

In the tapestry of consciousness, where dreams weave their intricate patterns and creativity flows like a river, we embrace the boundless horizons of the imagination and harness the transformative power of dreams to manifest our deepest aspirations and desires. Whether through visionary insights, symbolic imagery, or intuitive inspiration, dreams serve as portals to the infinite realms of creativity, inviting us to explore, create, and innovate with fearless abandon.

As you embark on your own journey of creative exploration, remember that the power to awaken the creative genius within lies within your reach—within the depths of your dreams, the expanses of your imagination, and the limitless horizons of your creative potential. Embrace the gifts that dreams offer, cultivate practices that honor the creative muse, and let your imagination soar to new heights of artistic expression and self-discovery. Awaken the creative genius within, and let the journey unfold.

Chapter 10

Practical Dreamwork Techniques

Dreams, like enigmatic puzzles waiting to be deciphered, offer glimpses into the depths of the subconscious mind, revealing hidden truths, unresolved emotions, and untapped potentials. In this chapter, we delve into the practical techniques of dreamwork, providing a step-by-step guide to interpreting your own dreams, exploring tools for dream analysis such as dream journals and group discussions, and presenting case studies of dream interpretation in practice.

Step-by-Step Guide to Interpreting Your Own Dreams

Interpreting dreams is an art as much as it is a science, requiring patience, intuition, and a willingness to explore the depths of the subconscious. While each dream is unique to the individual dreamer, certain principles and techniques can guide the process of dream analysis and unlock the hidden meanings embedded within dream symbolism. Here's a step-by-step guide to interpreting your own dreams:

Dream Recall: The first step in dream interpretation is to recall the details of your dream as soon as you awaken. Take a few moments to reflect on the imagery, emotions, and narrative of the dream, paying attention to any vivid or recurring symbols that stand out to you. Write down or record your dream in a dream journal, capturing as much detail as possible to aid in later analysis.

Symbol Identification: Identify key symbols and themes within your dream that carry personal significance or emotional resonance. Symbols may include people, animals, objects, or settings that evoke specific feelings or associations for you. Consider the context of each symbol within the dream narrative and reflect on its potential meanings and implications in relation to your waking life experiences and inner psychological landscape.

Emotional Exploration: Explore the emotions and feelings evoked by your dream, noting any predominant emotions or shifts in mood throughout the dream narrative. Pay attention to the intensity and quality of emotions experienced within the dream, as well as any unresolved emotional conflicts or tensions that may be reflected in the dream imagery. Emotions serve as valuable clues to the underlying themes and dynamics at play within the dream.

Narrative Analysis: Analyze the storyline and sequence of events within your dream, considering the overarching narrative structure and plot development. Look for patterns, motifs, and recurring themes that emerge throughout the dream, as well as any significant shifts or transitions in the dream narrative. Reflect on the underlying messages and insights conveyed through the symbolic language of the dream, and consider how they may relate to your waking life circumstances and inner psychological landscape.

Association and Amplification: Engage in free association and amplification techniques to explore the deeper layers of meaning embedded within dream symbolism. Allow your mind to wander freely and make spontaneous connections between dream symbols, personal experiences, memories, and emotions. Amplify the symbolic imagery of the dream by imagining it in vivid detail and exploring its potential associations and implications within the context of your life story and inner psychological dynamics.

Integration and Reflection: Reflect on the insights and revelations gained through the process of dream interpretation, considering how they may inform your understanding of yourself, your relationships, and your life path. Look for patterns and themes that recur across multiple dreams, as well as any transformative insights or resolutions that arise through dreamwork. Integrate the wisdom of your dreams into your waking life practices and personal growth journey, cultivating greater self-awareness, insight, and alignment with your deepest values and aspirations.

Tools for Dream Analysis

In addition to the steps outlined above, several tools and techniques can enhance the process of dream analysis and deepen your understanding of dream symbolism and meaning. Here are some tools for dream analysis:

Dream Journals: Dream journals serve as invaluable tools for recording and analyzing dream content, facilitating the process of dream recall and interpretation. Keep a notebook or digital journal by your bedside to capture the details of your dreams upon waking, including imagery, emotions, and narrative elements. Review your dream journal regularly to identify patterns, symbols, and themes that recur across multiple dreams, and reflect on their significance in relation to your waking life experiences and inner psychological landscape.

Symbol Dictionaries: Consult symbol dictionaries or dream interpretation guides to explore the meanings and associations of common dream symbols. While dream symbolism is highly personal and subjective, symbol dictionaries can provide helpful insights and prompts for reflection, sparking new perspectives on the symbolic imagery of your dreams. Keep in mind that dream symbols may carry different meanings for different individuals, depending on personal experiences, cultural backgrounds, and psychological dynamics.

Group Dreamwork: Participate in group dreamwork sessions or dream circles to share and explore dream content in a supportive and collaborative environment. Joining a dreamwork group allows you to gain fresh perspectives on your dreams, receive feedback and insights from others, and engage in dialogue about the symbolic language of dreams. Group dreamwork fosters a sense of community and connection, providing a space for mutual exploration and discovery of the dream world.

Artistic Expression: Expressing dream content through artistic mediums such as drawing, painting, or collage can deepen your engagement with dream symbolism and evoke intuitive insights and associations. Use art as a means of amplifying and exploring the imagery of your dreams, allowing the creative process to unfold organically and intuitively. Artistic expression can bypass the limitations of language and rational thought, tapping into the deeper layers of the subconscious and revealing hidden meanings and insights within dream symbolism.

Active Imagination: Practice active imagination techniques inspired by Jungian psychology to engage with dream imagery and symbols through creative expression. Enter into dialogue with dream characters, symbols, and scenarios as if they were living entities, allowing them to communicate their insights and wisdom to you. Write dialogues with dream characters, create visual representations of dream scenes, or embody dream symbolism through movement and gesture. By actively engaging with dream imagery, you deepen your connection to the subconscious and access the creative insights and inspiration that reside within.

Case Studies of Dream Interpretation in Practice

To illustrate the practical application of dreamwork techniques, let's explore two case studies of dream interpretation in practice:

Case Study 1: The Flying Elephant

Dream Content: A dreamer recalls a vivid dream in which they encounter an elephant with wings, soaring gracefully through the sky. The dreamer feels a sense of awe and wonder as they watch the flying elephant glide effortlessly through the clouds.

Symbol Analysis: The flying elephant symbolizes a powerful sense of freedom, liberation, and transcendence. Elephants are traditionally associated with strength, wisdom, and emotional intelligence, while wings symbolize the ability to transcend limitations and rise above earthly concerns. The dreamer's awe and wonder suggest a deep emotional resonance with the symbolism of the flying elephant, indicating a profound longing for freedom and self-expression.

Emotional Exploration: The dreamer's feelings of awe and wonder reflect a sense of awe and wonder reflect a deep emotional connection to the symbolism of the flying elephant, indicating a profound longing for freedom and self-expression. The dream may be tapping into the dreamer's unconscious desire to break free from limitations, soar to new heights, and embrace their full potential.

Narrative Analysis: The narrative of the dream revolves around the theme of freedom and transcendence, as symbolized by the flying elephant. The dreamer is drawn to the image of the flying elephant, captivated by its grace and beauty as it soars through the sky. The dream may be signaling a desire to break free from constraints, expand horizons, and explore new possibilities in life.

Association and Amplification: The dreamer explores the symbolism of the flying elephant through free association and amplification techniques, making connections between the dream imagery and personal experiences. They reflect on times in their life when they felt constrained or limited, as well as moments of liberation and empowerment. The flying elephant becomes a symbol of their inner strength, resilience, and capacity for transformation.

Integration and Reflection: The dreamer reflects on the insights and revelations gained through the process of dream interpretation, considering how they can apply these insights to their waking life experiences. They recognize the need to cultivate a sense of freedom and self-expression in their life, embracing opportunities for growth and exploration. The dream serves as a reminder to embrace their innate power and soar to new heights of creativity and self-discovery.

Case Study 2: The Lost Child

Dream Content: A dreamer recounts a recurring dream in which they are searching for a lost child in a crowded city. Despite their frantic efforts to find the child, they are unable to locate them, experiencing feelings of anxiety and desperation.

Symbol Analysis: The lost child symbolizes a sense of vulnerability, innocence, and inner needs that have been neglected or overlooked. The crowded city represents the complexities and distractions of modern life, while the dreamer's frantic search reflects a deep-seated fear of losing touch with their inner child and authentic self.

Emotional Exploration: The dreamer's feelings of anxiety and desperation reflect a sense of disconnection from their inner needs and emotional well-being. The dream may be highlighting unresolved feelings of insecurity, inadequacy, or abandonment that require attention and nurturing.

Narrative Analysis: The narrative of the dream centers around the theme of lost innocence and the search for emotional fulfillment. The dreamer's inability to locate the lost child mirrors a sense of disorientation and confusion in their waking life, as they struggle to find a sense of purpose and belonging amidst the chaos and pressures of society.

Association and Amplification: The dreamer explores the symbolism of the lost child through free association and amplification techniques, reflecting on their own experiences of childhood, parental relationships, and emotional needs. They recognize patterns of neglect or abandonment that may have contributed to feelings of insecurity and fear in their adult life, as well as opportunities for healing and self-compassion.

Integration and Reflection: The dreamer reflects on the insights and revelations gained through the process of dream interpretation, considering how they can apply these insights to their waking life experiences. They recognize the need to nurture their inner child and cultivate a sense of emotional well-being and self-acceptance. The dream serves as a catalyst for inner growth and healing, empowering the dreamer to reclaim lost innocence and embrace their authentic self.

Through the practice of dreamwork techniques such as symbol analysis, emotional exploration, narrative analysis, association and amplification, and integration and reflection, dreamers can unlock the hidden meanings and insights embedded within their dreams, gaining a deeper understanding of themselves and their life journey.

Unlocking the Wisdom of the Dream World

As we conclude our exploration of practical dreamwork techniques, we are reminded of the transformative power of dreams to illuminate the path of self-discovery, insight, and personal growth. By engaging in the process of dream analysis with curiosity, openness, and reverence, dreamers unlock the hidden wisdom and insights that reside within the dream landscape, gaining a deeper understanding of themselves and their life journey.

Dreams serve as portals to the depths of the subconscious mind, offering glimpses into the hidden realms of the psyche and revealing the intricate tapestry of thoughts, emotions, and experiences that shape our waking reality. Through the practice of dreamwork techniques, dreamers embark on a journey of exploration and discovery, unraveling the symbolic language of dreams and integrating their insights into their waking life practices and personal growth journey.

As you embark on your own journey of dreamwork, remember to approach the process with patience, curiosity, and self-compassion, trusting in the transformative power of dreams to guide you on the path of self-discovery and insight. Embrace the wisdom of the dream world, and let the journey unfold.

Chapter 11

Advanced Topics in Dream Interpretation

In the intricate tapestry of human consciousness, dreams serve as portals to the depths of the psyche, offering insights, revelations, and transformative experiences that transcend the boundaries of waking reality. In this chapter, we delve into advanced topics in dream interpretation, exploring the role of dreams in various spiritual traditions, examining the concept of prophetic and precognitive dreams, and investigating the intersection of dreams with psychological therapy.

The Role of Dreams in Various Spiritual Traditions

Across cultures and throughout history, dreams have held sacred significance as vehicles for spiritual revelation, divine guidance, and mystical experience. From ancient civilizations to modern-day religious traditions, dreams have played a central role in shaping religious beliefs, practices, and rituals. Here are some examples of the role of dreams in various spiritual traditions:

Ancient Egypt: In ancient Egypt, dreams were regarded as messages from the gods and ancestors, offering insights into the divine will and guidance for the living. The Egyptian Book of the Dead contains instructions for interpreting dreams and navigating the journey of the soul through the afterlife.

Judeo-Christian Tradition: In the Judeo-Christian tradition, dreams are depicted as a means of divine communication, with numerous biblical figures receiving prophetic dreams and visions. For example, Joseph's dream of interpreting Pharaoh's dreams in the book of Genesis played a pivotal role in shaping the destiny of the Israelites.

Greek Mythology: In Greek mythology, dreams were believed to be messages from the gods, delivered through the medium of Morpheus, the god of dreams. The Oracle at Delphi often interpreted dreams as omens and portents of future events, guiding individuals in matters of personal and collective significance.

Indigenous Traditions: Many indigenous cultures view dreams as a sacred means of connecting with the spirit world and receiving guidance from ancestors and spirit guides. Dreaming ceremonies and rituals are often used to facilitate communication with the spirit realm and gain insights into healing, prophecy, and communal harmony.

Tibetan Buddhism: In Tibetan Buddhism, dreams are seen as a reflection of the mind's innate wisdom and enlightenment potential. Dream yoga practices involve training the mind to maintain awareness and lucidity during the dream state, allowing practitioners to gain insight into the nature of reality and achieve spiritual awakening.

Exploring the Concept of Prophetic and Precognitive Dreams

Prophetic and precognitive dreams are those that seem to foretell future events or offer insights into unfolding circumstances beyond the realm of ordinary perception. While skeptics may dismiss such experiences as mere coincidence or wishful thinking, proponents of these phenomena point to compelling anecdotal evidence and scientific studies that suggest a deeper, unexplained connection between dreams and future events. Here are some key considerations when exploring the concept of prophetic and precognitive dreams:

Subjective Experience: Prophetic and precognitive dreams are highly subjective experiences that defy conventional explanations and scientific scrutiny. While some individuals report vivid dreams that accurately predict future events, others may dismiss such experiences as fantastical or delusional. The subjective nature of these phenomena makes them difficult to study empirically and open to interpretation.

Symbolic Language: Prophetic and precognitive dreams often communicate through the symbolic language of dreams, using metaphor, imagery, and emotion to convey insights and impressions about future events. Interpreting the symbolic meaning of these dreams requires careful attention to context, personal associations, and intuitive insights that may not be immediately apparent.

Cultural and Religious Beliefs: Belief in prophetic and precognitive dreams varies widely across cultures and religious traditions, with some societies embracing these phenomena as evidence of divine guidance or supernatural insight, while others dismiss them as superstitious or irrational. Cultural and religious beliefs play a significant role in shaping individual interpretations of prophetic dreams and the value assigned to them within a given society.

Scientific Research: While empirical evidence for the existence of prophetic and precognitive dreams remains elusive, some scientific studies have explored the possibility of predictive dreaming through controlled experiments and statistical analysis. While the results of such studies are mixed and inconclusive, they have sparked ongoing debate and speculation about the nature of consciousness and the potential limits of human perception.

Personal Validation: For individuals who have experienced prophetic or precognitive dreams firsthand, the subjective validation of these experiences can be profound and life-changing. Whether through dreams that forewarn of impending danger, provide guidance in times of uncertainty, or offer glimpses into future possibilities, the personal significance of these experiences cannot be easily dismissed or explained away.

The Intersection of Dreams with Psychological Therapy

In addition to their spiritual and metaphysical significance, dreams play a central role in psychological therapy and the process of self-discovery and healing. From the pioneering work of Sigmund Freud and Carl Jung to contemporary approaches such as dream analysis and dreamwork techniques, dreams offer valuable insights into the unconscious mind and the underlying dynamics of psychological and emotional well-being. Here are some ways in which dreams intersect with psychological therapy:

Freudian Dream Analysis: Sigmund Freud, the founder of psychoanalysis, viewed dreams as the "royal road to the unconscious," offering glimpses into repressed desires, fears, and conflicts that shape behavior and personality. Freudian dream analysis involves uncovering latent content beneath the manifest content of dreams, exploring hidden wishes, anxieties, and unresolved conflicts through techniques such as free association and interpretation of dream symbolism.

Jungian Dreamwork: Carl Jung expanded upon Freud's theories of dream analysis, emphasizing the symbolic and archetypal dimensions of dreams as expressions of the collective unconscious. Jungian dreamwork involves engaging with dream imagery, symbols, and themes to explore the deeper layers of the psyche and facilitate individuation—the process of integrating unconscious elements into conscious awareness. Techniques such as active imagination, amplification, and dream dialogue are used to elucidate the meaning and significance of dream content.

Dream Therapy: In contemporary psychology, dream therapy approaches such as Gestalt dreamwork, cognitive-behavioral therapy (CBT) for nightmares, and integrative dreamwork combine elements of psychotherapy with dream analysis techniques to promote emotional healing, self-awareness, and personal growth. Dream therapy may involve exploring recurring themes, processing traumatic experiences, or gaining insight into relationship dynamics and life transitions through the lens of dream symbolism.

Dreams as Metaphors for Healing: Dreams often serve as metaphors for psychological and emotional processes that are unfolding within the individual's inner landscape. Dreams may offer symbolic representations of unresolved conflicts, unmet needs, or untapped potentials, providing a safe and creative space for exploring and integrating these aspects of the self. By engaging with dream imagery and symbolism in therapy, individuals can gain insight into unconscious patterns and develop strategies for positive change and self-empowerment.

Integration of Dreamwork with Therapeutic Modalities: Many therapists integrate dreamwork techniques with other therapeutic modalities such as mindfulness-based therapy, somatic experiencing, and expressive arts therapy to enhance the therapeutic process and facilitate holistic healing. Dreamwork may be used as a complementary tool for deepening self-awareness, accessing unconscious material, and fostering resilience and self-compassion in the face of adversity.

Navigating the Depths of the Dream World

As we navigate the depths of the dream world and explore advanced topics in dream interpretation, we are reminded of the profound significance of dreams as gateways to the mysteries of the psyche, the cosmos, and the human experience. Whether viewed through the lens of spirituality, metaphysics, psychology, or therapy, dreams offer a rich tapestry of insights, revelations, and transformative experiences that invite us to explore the depths of our inner landscape and awaken to the infinite possibilities that reside within.

By embracing the multidimensional nature of dreams and cultivating practices of dream interpretation, exploration, and integration, we unlock the hidden wisdom and healing potential that lies within the dream landscape. Whether through prophetic visions, spiritual revelations, or psychological insights, dreams serve as guiding lights on the journey of self-discovery, self-awareness, and self-realization, illuminating the path of transformation and awakening for those willing to embark on the adventure of dreamwork.

As you continue your exploration of the dream world and delve into the mysteries of the unconscious mind, remember to approach the journey with curiosity, openness, and reverence, trusting in the wisdom and guidance that dreams offer as we navigate the depths of the psyche and awaken to the infinite possibilities that reside within. Let your dreams be your companions, your teachers, and your allies on the path of self-discovery and transformation, and may they illuminate the way forward with clarity, insight, and grace.

Chapter 12

Conclusion

Embracing the Wisdom of Dreams

Throughout the journey of dream exploration, we have embarked on a fascinating odyssey into the depths of the human psyche, uncovering the hidden realms of the subconscious mind and unlocking the transformative power of dreams. From ancient civilizations to modern-day psychology, dreams have captivated the imagination and inspired awe, offering insights, revelations, and guidance that transcend the boundaries of waking reality. As we conclude our exploration of the dream world, let us reflect on the lessons learned, the wisdom gained, and the infinite possibilities that lie ahead on the path of dreamwork and self-discovery.

Summarizing the Journey of Dream Exploration

Our journey into the world of dreams has been a journey of discovery, illumination, and self-awareness, as we navigated the labyrinthine landscapes of the subconscious mind and unraveled the symbolic language of dreams. We began by exploring the allure of dreams and their historical significance, delving into the rich tapestry of dream interpretation through the ages and uncovering the hidden meanings and messages encoded within the fabric of dream symbolism. We then ventured into the science of dreaming, gaining insights into the neural mechanisms of sleep, the stages of the sleep cycle, and the latest research on the function and purpose of dreams.

Next, we embarked on a voyage through the annals of dream interpretation, tracing the evolution of dream analysis from ancient civilizations to modern-day psychology, and exploring the pioneering work of Freud, Jung, and other significant figures in the field. We delved into the common themes and symbols that populate the dream landscape, examining their cultural variations and psychological significance, and discovering the profound insights and revelations that dreams offer as windows to the subconscious mind.

We then turned our attention to the language of dreams, exploring the role of metaphor and symbolism in dream imagery, and learning how to recognize and interpret personal symbols and their meanings. We explored the emotional language of dreams, deciphering the underlying feelings and conflicts that shape dream narratives, and uncovering the hidden truths and unspoken desires that reside within the depths of the psyche.

As our journey progressed, we ventured into the realm of lucid dreaming, learning how to take control of the dream world and harness its creative potential for self-discovery and problem-solving. We explored the healing power of dreams, discovering how disturbing dreams and nightmares can serve as catalysts for growth and transformation, and learning strategies for coping with and interpreting these challenging experiences.

We then delved into the intersection of dreams with creativity, discovering how dreams inspire artistic expression and fuel the creative process, and learning techniques for incubating and harnessing creative dreams for personal and professional endeavors. Finally, we explored practical dreamwork techniques, gaining insights into the process of dream interpretation, exploring tools for dream analysis, and examining case studies of dream interpretation in practice.

Integrating Dreamwork into Daily Life for Personal Growth

As we conclude our journey of dream exploration, we are reminded that the wisdom of dreams is not confined to the realm of sleep, but can be integrated into our daily lives for personal growth, insight, and transformation. By incorporating dreamwork practices into our daily routine, we cultivate greater self-awareness, deepen our connection to the subconscious mind, and unlock the hidden potentials that lie within.

One way to integrate dreamwork into daily life is to keep a dream journal and record our dreams upon waking. By capturing the details of our dreams and reflecting on their symbolism and significance, we gain valuable insights into our inner world and the dynamics that shape our thoughts, feelings, and behaviors. Regular journaling allows us to track patterns, themes, and recurring symbols across multiple dreams, providing a roadmap for self-discovery and personal growth.

Another way to integrate dream work into daily life is to engage in dream analysis and reflection throughout the day. By taking time to revisit our dreams, explore their meanings, and connect them to our waking life experiences, we deepen our understanding of ourselves and gain fresh perspectives on the challenges and opportunities that arise in our lives. Dreamwork can be incorporated into daily mindfulness practices such as meditation, visualization, and creative expression, allowing us to access the wisdom of dreams and integrate it into our conscious awareness.

Dreamwork can also be integrated into therapeutic practices and self-care routines, providing a powerful tool for healing, insight, and self-discovery. By exploring dream imagery, symbolism, and themes in therapy sessions or support groups, we can gain valuable insights into unconscious patterns and dynamics, and develop strategies for positive change and personal empowerment. Dreamwork can also be used as a tool for self-care and stress management, providing a source of inspiration, guidance, and renewal in times of challenge and adversity.

Encouragement for Continued Exploration of the Dream World

As we conclude our journey of dream exploration, let us remember that the adventure does not end here, but continues on as an ongoing quest for self-discovery, insight, and transformation. The world of dreams is a vast and mysterious realm, filled with endless possibilities and infinite wisdom waiting to be uncovered. By embracing the wisdom of dreams and continuing to explore their depths, we open ourselves to new experiences, new insights, and new horizons of understanding.

Let us remain open to the messages and revelations that dreams offer, trusting in the wisdom of the subconscious mind to guide us on our journey of self-discovery and personal growth. Let us cultivate practices of dreamwork and reflection, integrating the wisdom of dreams into our daily lives and harnessing their transformative power for positive change and self-empowerment.

As we venture forth into the unknown territories of the dream world, let us do so with curiosity, courage, and an open heart, knowing that the path of dream exploration is a journey of endless possibility and infinite wonder. May we continue to explore the depths of the psyche, unlock the mysteries of the subconscious mind, and awaken to the boundless potential that lies within.

In the words of the poet Rumi, "The dream is a hidden door in the innermost and most secret recesses of the soul, opening into that cosmic night which was psyche long before there was any ego-consciousness, and which will remain psyche no matter how far our ego-consciousness may extend." May we embrace the wisdom of dreams and journey into the depths of the soul, guided by the light of awareness and the wisdom of the unconscious mind.

Chapter 13

Appendices

In this appendices section, you will find valuable resources and tools to support your ongoing exploration of dreams and dream interpretation. From a dream symbol dictionary for quick reference to templates for a dream journal and resources for further study, these appendices are designed to enhance your understanding and practice of dreamwork.

Dream Symbol Dictionary

Dream symbolism is a rich and intricate language that communicates through imagery, metaphor, and emotion. This dream symbol dictionary provides a quick reference guide to common dream symbols and their potential meanings. Keep in mind that dream interpretation is highly subjective and can vary based on personal associations, cultural background, and individual experiences.

Common Dream Symbols (Categories)

Animals:

Bear: Strength, power, protection.

Cat: Independence, intuition, mystery.

Dog: Loyalty, friendship, companionship.

Eagle: Freedom, vision, spiritual enlightenment.

Fish: Abundance, fertility, unconscious emotions.

Horse: Freedom, power, instinctual energy.

Snake: Transformation, healing, hidden fears.

Wolf: Instinct, intelligence, social connection.

Objects:

Key: Unlocking potential, and access to hidden knowledge.

Mirror: Self-reflection, self-awareness, inner truth.

Book: Wisdom, knowledge, learning.

Clock: Time, deadlines, urgency.

Door: Opportunities, transitions, new beginnings.

Tree: Growth, vitality, connection to nature.

Bridge: Transition, connection between worlds.

House: Self, identity, sense of security.

Emotions:

Joy: Happiness, contentment, fulfillment.

Fear: Anxiety, insecurity, unresolved issues.

Anger: Frustration, conflict, repressed emotions.

Sadness: Grief, loss, emotional healing.

Love: Connection, intimacy, acceptance.

Confusion: Uncertainty, lack of clarity, inner conflict.

Excitement: Anticipation, enthusiasm, motivation.

Peace: Calmness, serenity, inner harmony.

Nature:

Sun: Vitality, energy, consciousness.

Moon: Intuition, emotions, feminine energy.

Stars: Inspiration, guidance, cosmic connection.

Water: Emotions, purification, renewal.

Fire: Passion, transformation, creativity.

Earth: Stability, grounding, nurturing energy.

Wind: Change, movement, freedom.

Rain: Cleansing, emotional release, renewal.

Actions:

Flying: Freedom, liberation, transcendence.

Falling: Loss of control, insecurity, fear of failure.

Chasing: Pursuit of goals, avoidance of problems.

Running: Escape, avoidance, pursuit of desires.

Dancing: Celebration, joy, self-expression.

Fighting: Conflict, confrontation, inner struggle.

Swimming: Emotions, exploration, adaptation.

Climbing: Overcoming obstacles, personal growth.

Common Dream Symbols (Alphabetical)

A

Abandonment - feeling neglected or rejected in waking life.

Acrobat - adaptability, flexibility, or balance.

Airplane - aspirations, freedom, or escape.

Angel - protection, guidance, or spiritual intervention.

Apple - temptation, knowledge, or desires.

B

Baby - innocence, vulnerability, or new beginnings.

Bridge - transitions, connections, or growth.

Butterfly - transformation, metamorphosis, or personal growth.

C

Candle - illumination, guidance, or spiritual insight.

Castle - strength, security, or isolation.

Cat - intuition, independence, or mystery.

Clock - passage of time, deadlines, or cycles.

D

Dancing - joy, celebration, or self-expression.

Darkness - fear, uncertainty, or the unknown.

Death - endings, transitions, or transformation.

Door - opportunities, choices, or new beginnings.

E

Eagle - vision, clarity, or perspective.

Elephant - strength, wisdom, or memory.

Eye - perception, awareness, or insight.

F

Fire - passion, transformation, or destruction.

Fish - intuition, creativity, or abundance.

Flower - beauty, growth, or femininity.

Flying - freedom, ambition, or transcendence.

G

Garden - growth, fertility, or abundance.

Ghost - unresolved emotions, memories, or fears.

Gold - wealth, value, or inner riches.

H

Horse - power, freedom, or vitality.

House - self, family, or security.

Hurricane - chaos, upheaval, or emotional turmoil.

I

Island - isolation, self-discovery, or tranquility.

Ice - frozen emotions, stagnation, or preservation.

Insects - irritations, annoyances, or transformation.

J

Journey - exploration, adventure, or personal growth.

Jail - restriction, confinement, or guilt.

Jewelry - self-worth, adornment, or status.

K

Key - access, opportunity, or secrets.

Knife - aggression, cutting ties, or fear.

L

Labyrinth - confusion, complexity, or self-discovery.

Lightning - sudden insight, illumination, or danger.

Lion - strength, courage, or leadership.

Love - affection, connection, or harmony.

M

Mirror - reflection, self-awareness, or introspection.

Moon - feminine energy, intuition, or cycles.

Mountain - challenges, obstacles, or transcendence.

Music - harmony, emotions, or expression.

N

Nightmare - anxiety, fear, or unresolved issues.

Necklace - adornment, beauty, or significance.

Numbers - order, significance, or patterns.

O

Ocean - emotions, vastness, or the unconscious.

Owl - wisdom, intuition, or mystery.

Orphan - feeling abandoned, alone, or disconnected.

P

Pregnancy - new beginnings, creativity, or growth.

Pyramid - stability, hierarchy, or spiritual ascent.

Painting - creativity, expression, or interpretation.

Q

Queen - femininity, authority, or leadership.

Quicksand - feeling trapped, sinking, or overwhelmed.

R

Rainbow - hope, promise, or diversity.

River - flow, emotions, or journey.

Rose - love, beauty, or passion.

Running - escape, urgency, or motivation.

S

Snake - transformation, temptation, or fear.

Spider - creativity, connection, or manipulation.

Storm - turmoil, chaos, or emotional intensity.

Sword - power, protection, or conflict.

T

Tree - growth, stability, or connection to nature.

Train - direction, journey, or progress.

Teeth - health, confidence, or communication.

Tomb - death, endings, or buried emotions.

U

Unicorn - magic, purity, or uniqueness.

UFO - mystery, otherworldly experiences, or fear of the unknown.

Underground - subconscious, hidden aspects, or secrets.

V

Volcano - eruption, passion, or repressed emotions.

Vampire - seduction, addiction, or fear of loss of vitality.

Violin - harmony, emotion, or creativity.

W

Waterfall - release, purification, or overwhelm.

Window - opportunities, perspective, or barriers.

Wolf - instinct, loyalty, or independence.

X

X-ray - insight, transparency, or seeing through illusions.

Xylophone - harmony, creativity, or playfulness.

Y

Yarn - connection, interdependence, or unraveling.

Yeti - fear of the unknown, isolation, or mystery.

Z

Zebra - balance, duality, or uniqueness.

Zombie - stagnation, mindlessness, or feeling overwhelmed.

Templates for a Dream Journal

Keeping a dream journal is an invaluable practice for recording and analyzing your dreams, facilitating the process of dream recall and interpretation, and gaining insights into your inner world. Use these templates to create your own dream journal and capture the details of your dreams upon waking.

Dream Journal Name:

Date:

Time of Dream:

Location:

Emotions Felt:

Key Symbols/Themes:

Narrative Summary:

Insights/Reflections:

Dream Analysis Template:

Dream Title:

Key Symbols/Themes:

Emotional Tone:

Interpretation/Analysis:

Connections to Waking Life:

Action Steps/Integration:

Lucid Dreaming Template:

Date:

Techniques Used:

Level of Lucidity:

Dream Environment:

Actions Taken:

Insights/Reflections:

Goals for Future Lucid Dreams:

Resources for Further Study on Dreams and Dream Interpretation

Expand your knowledge and deepen your understanding of dreams and dream interpretation with these recommended resources:

Books:

"The Interpretation of Dreams" by Sigmund Freud

"Man and His Symbols" by Carl Jung

"Inner Work: Using Dreams and Active Imagination for Personal Growth" by Robert A. Johnson

"The Dreamer's Dictionary" by Stearn Robinson and Tom Corbett

"Dreams: A Portal to the Source" by Edward C. Whitmont

Online Courses:

"Dream Interpretation and Symbolism" on Udemy

"The Science of Dreaming" on Coursera

"Lucid Dreaming: Gateway to the Inner Self" by Robert Waggoner on lucidacademy.com

Websites and Blogs:

DreamMoods.com: A comprehensive online resource for dream interpretation and symbolism.

LucidDreaming.com: Offers articles, tutorials, and resources on lucid dreaming and dream exploration.

The International Association for the Study of Dreams (IASD): Provides information on conferences, publications, and research in the field of dream studies.

Podcasts:

"The Dream Show" by The Dream Tribe

"The Dreaming Collective" by Dr. Clare Johnson

"Dreams Unzipped" by Kelly Sullivan Walden

By exploring these resources and incorporating dreamwork practices into your daily life, you can deepen your connection to the wisdom of dreams, unlock the secrets of the subconscious mind, and embark on a journey of self-discovery and personal growth that transcends the boundaries of waking reality. Happy dreaming!